D1521533

Properties of Matter

Contents

Contents

1 What Makes Up Matter?

Matter is something that has mass and takes up space. Matter can be a solid, a liquid, or a gas.

Looking at Matter

When you look around, you may see things like desks and people. You may feel things you cannot see, like air blowing across your face. Desks, people, and blowing air are examples of matter. **Matter** is anything that has mass and takes up space.

Properties are special qualities for which something is known. Matter has many different properties, such as color, size, shape, and the way it feels. It is easy to see some properties of matter. You may need to use a microscope or hand lens to see other properties.

feather

cloth

People use microscopes to make objects look larger. This makes it easier to see an object's properties of matter. Objects can look very different under a microscope.

Using powerful microscopes, scientists have learned that all matter is made up of very tiny pieces called particles. The particles are always moving.

The smallest particle of matter that has the same properties of that matter is called an **atom** (AT uhm). All objects are made up of many, many atoms. In fact, there are billions of atoms in a tiny piece of sand!

Most matter is made up of atoms that have joined with other atoms to make a molecule (MAHL ih kyool). A **molecule** is one particle of matter that is made up of two or more atoms joined together. A particle of water is a molecule made up of three atoms.

shampoo

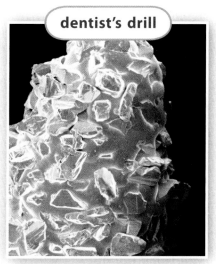

dentist's drill

What states of water does this picture show?

Three States of Matter

Matter comes in different forms, or states. The states of matter are three forms that matter usually takes: solid, liquid, and gas.

Water looks very different in its three states of matter. Ice is a solid. Water in a pool is a liquid. Water vapor is a gas, which you cannot see. The three states of water look different, but they are all the same kind of matter. Each particle of ice, water, and water vapor is made up of the same kind of molecule. Each molecule is made up of the same three kinds of atoms.

Why do solids, liquids, and gases have different properties? The particles of matter in each of these states are put together in different ways. Look at the chart to understand how.

States of Matter: Water

State of Matter	Molecules	Diagram
Solid The ice frozen on the ground is a solid.	Molecules in a solid are packed close together in a regular pattern.	
Liquid The water in a lake is a liquid.	Molecules in a liquid slide past each other but stay close together. They do not form a regular pattern.	
Water vapor The water vapor in the air is a gas.	Molecules in a gas move quickly and do not stay close together. They do not form any pattern.	

Liquid water inside the tea kettle changes to water vapor, a gas that you cannot see above the spout. The steam that you can see is not a gas. It is made of tiny drops of water mixed with air.

Properties of Solids, Liquids, and Gases

How do you know that water is inside this tea kettle? The steam you see coming from the spout is a clue. Water turns to steam. Matter can change from one state to another, but it does not become a new kind of matter. The state of matter is a physical property (FIHZ ih kuhl PRAHP ur tee) of matter. A **physical property** of matter can be seen without changing matter into something new. Size, shape, color, and the way something feels are other physical properties of matter.

You can use the table below to understand the physical properties of solids, liquids, and gases. Remember this about the shapes of different states of matter: A solid always keeps its own shape. A liquid takes the shape of the container it is in. A gas spreads apart or can be squeezed together to fit into spaces.

States of Matter

State of Matter	Shape	Size
Solid	Definite shape	Fixed size
Liquid	No definite shape	Fixed size
Gas	No definite shape	No fixed size

MAIN IDEA

How are ice, water, and water vapor alike?

2

How Is Matter Measured?

People use the metric system to measure objects. You can measure objects to find their mass and volume.

The Metric System

Years ago, people came up with a measurement system that everyone could use to measure in the same way. This measurement system helps people talk about matter. The system is called the metric system (MEHT rihk SIHS tuhm). The **metric system** is a system of measurement that uses multiples of 10. Look at the chart on the next page to see how different metric units work together.

Many giraffes grow to be more than 5.5 m tall. How can you find out how tall a giraffe is? You measure it!

A metric ruler measures length in centimeters (cm).

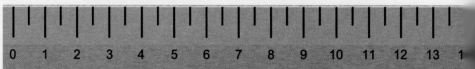

Metric Units Conversion Chart

Type of Measurement	Metric Unit	Converts To
Length	1 centimeter (cm)	10 millimeters (mm)
	1 meter (m)	100 centimeters (cm)
	1 kilometer (km)	1,000 meters (m)
Volume	1 liter (L)	1,000 milliliters (mL)
Mass	1 kilogram (kg)	1,000 grams (g)

On the chart, find the metric units centimeter, meter, and kilometer. These metric units are used to measure length. You can see that 100 centimeters is the same as 1 meter, and 1,000 meters is the same as 1 kilometer. The numbers 100 and 1,000 are multiples of 10. You can change—or convert—to different metric units simply by multiplying or dividing by a multiple of 10.

To measure objects, people use tools that measure in metric units such as centimeters, liters, or kilograms. Length or height can be measured with a ruler that shows centimeters or meters. Mass can be measured using a balance that shows grams or kilograms. The volume of liquids can be measured with a container that shows milliliters or liters.

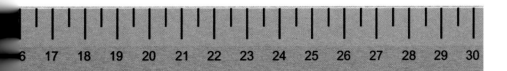

Mass

Think about holding two blocks, one in each hand. They are the same size, color, and shape. However, one block feels heavier than the other. To find the difference between the blocks, you can measure their masses. **Mass** is the amount of matter in an object. The block that feels heavier has more mass—and more matter.

All kinds of matter have mass. Mass is a physical property that tells more about an object. Knowing the masses of different objects helps people understand them and sort them into groups. You can use a tool called a balance to measure mass.

This girl is using a balance to measure the mass of a block.

To measure the mass of a block, you put it on one pan of a balance. Then you add objects called standards to the other pan. Standards are objects with known masses. For example, a 1-gram standard has a mass of exactly 1 gram. A 1-kilogram standard has a mass of exactly 1 kilogram.

As you add standards to the other pan of the balance, you watch to see when the two pans balance. When the pans balance, the total mass of the standards is the same as the mass of the block.

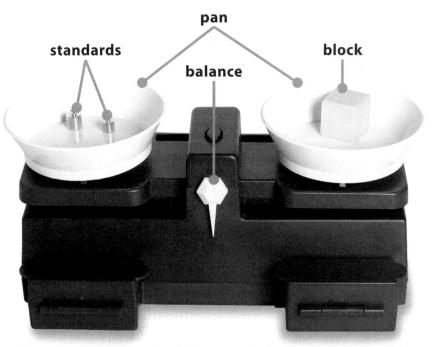

pan

standards

block

balance

The standards on the left pan of the balance have the same total mass as the block on the right pan.

To find the volume of a solid like this one, you multiply its length times its width, times its height.

4 cm x 4 cm x 4 cm = 64 cm³

You can use a container called a beaker to measure the volume of a liquid.

Volume

Another physical property of matter that can be measured is volume (VAHL yoom). **Volume** is the amount of space that matter takes up. All matter— even air and tiny particles—has mass and volume.

Volume can be measured in different ways. To find the volume of a liquid, you use a measurement container such as a beaker. The volume of a liquid is measured in the metric units liters (L) and milliliters (ml).

To find the volume of a rectangular solid, such as a block, you multiply the length, width, and height of the block. The volume of a solid is measured in cubic centimeters (cm^3).

How do you measure the volume of a solid with a strange shape, such as a rock? First, you put some water in a beaker and write down the volume of the liquid. Then you place the rock into the beaker. The volume of liquid will now be greater. Write down the new water volume.

The change in water volume is the same as the volume of the rock. One milliliter has the same volume as one cubic centimeter. This means that if the water volume in the beaker goes up by 50 milliliters, the volume of the rock is 50 cm^3.

A beaker of water can help you measure the volume of some objects.

Weight

How much does this bear cub weigh? Is its weight (wayt) the same as its mass? No. Mass is the amount of matter in an object. **Weight** is the measure of the pull of gravity on an object.

The bear's mass is the same everywhere it goes. The bear's weight will change as the bear moves to different places on Earth. This is because the amount of gravity pulling on the bear is different in different places.

A spring scale can measure the weight of a bear cub.

At sea level, the bear's weight is a little bit more than its weight on the top of a high mountain. This is because the pull of gravity is stronger at sea level than it is on the top of a mountain. When the bear moves to the top of a mountain, it is farther from the center of Earth. The bear's weight is less on the mountain top because the pull of gravity is weaker there.

On the Moon, the pull of gravity is very weak. A bear would weigh much less on the Moon than it does anywhere on Earth.

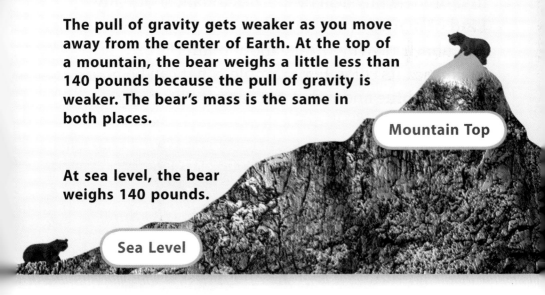

The pull of gravity gets weaker as you move away from the center of Earth. At the top of a mountain, the bear weighs a little less than 140 pounds because the pull of gravity is weaker. The bear's mass is the same in both places.

Mountain Top

At sea level, the bear weighs 140 pounds.

Sea Level

DRAW CONCLUSIONS

How can you find the volume of a block?

3 What Are Physical and Chemical Properties?

Matter has physical and chemical properties. People use physical and chemical properties to describe and sort different types of matter.

Physical Properties

In the morning you might bring your blue backpack to school. At lunch you might eat a big, smooth apple. At night you might sleep on a soft pillow. The words "blue," "big," "smooth," and "soft" all tell about physical properties of matter. You can use physical properties to talk about any kind of matter.

Color One way to talk about matter is by looking at its color. For example, a hat can be blue or red or blue and red. A hat can also be many different colors.

Some Physical Properties

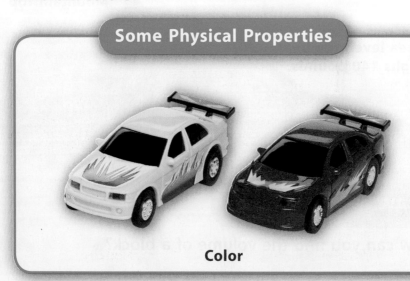

Color

Shape Another way to talk about matter is by looking at its shape. Some things have shapes that are easy to name. The two shapes shown in the picture are a cube and a cylinder. Many things do not have a shape that is easy to talk about. It might be hard to name the shape of objects like your hand, a butterfly, or a leaf.

Texture The texture (TEHKS chur) of an object tells how the object feels. Glass windows have a smooth texture. The trunk of a tree may have a bumpy texture. Luster tells how the outside of an object looks when light shines on it. A mirror is very shiny, but a piece of black paper is not shiny. The two rocks in the picture have different textures. One is smooth. The other is rough.

Shape   Texture

Density Another physical property of matter is density (DEHN sih tee). **Density** tells how much matter is in a certain space, or volume. For example, one cubic centimeter of rock has more mass than one cubic centimeter of cotton. That means that rock is more dense than cotton.

The density of an object makes it float or sink in a liquid like water. If something is more dense than water, it will sink. If it is less dense than water, it will float.

Different Densities

OIL This liquid has the lowest density. It is on top.

WATER This liquid has the middle density.

CORN SYRUP This liquid has the highest density. It is on the bottom.

Which of these solid objects is the most dense? Why?

Useful Physical Properties

Each kind of matter has its own set of physical properties. These physical properties help people choose how to use each kind of matter.

You would not use ice to make a chair. It would melt in a warm room. The physical properties of wood and metal make these kinds of matter better for making a chair. The chair would be strong and it would keep its shape in a warm or cold room.

Physical properties that make matter useful in one way do not always make it useful in another way. Glass is clear and smooth. Its physical properties make it useful for making windows. But glass would not be useful for making safety glasses. It breaks too easily.

This desk top is made from foam rubber.
What will happen when the boy puts the books on it?

Chemical Properties

Look at the pictures of the burnt log and the cut log. The logs have different physical properties, such as size, shape, and texture.

You cannot burn a burnt log, but you can burn a cut log. Something that can be burned has a property of matter called a chemical (KEHM ih kuhl) property. A **chemical property** can be seen only when matter is changed into a new kind of matter. You can see the chemical property of wood as it burns and becomes ash. Ash is a different kind of matter than wood.

Cut logs can burn. They have a chemical property because they can change into a different kind of matter by burning.

Burnt logs—or ash—cannot burn again. They do not have the chemical property that allows them to burn.

Describing Chemical Properties

When you cook an egg in a frying pan, heat changes the raw egg into something different—a cooked egg. The fact that the egg can change into a new kind of matter when it is heated is a chemical property. The heat does not change the pan into new matter. It just warms the pan. The pan has had a physical change, not a chemical change.

Matter can change in different ways when it meets air, heat, and water. Chemical properties can help you sort matter into groups. Some metal will get rusty when it gets wet, but it will not burn. Wood will not get rusty, but it will burn easily. Metal and wood do not have the same chemical properties.

When you cook an egg, new matter forms.

COMPARE AND CONTRAST

How is a chemical property differe from aphysical property?

Glossary

atom (AT uhm) The smallest particle of matter that has the properties of that matter.

chemical property (KEHM ih kuhl PRAP ur tee) A characteristic of matter that can be observed only when matter is changed into a new kind of matter.

density (DEHN sih tee) The amount of matter in a given space, or a given volume.

mass (mas) The amount of matter in an object.

matter (MAT ur) Anything that has mass and takes up space.

metric system (EHT rihk SIHS tuhm) A system of measurement based on multiples of 10.

Glossary

molecule (MAHL ih kyool) A single particle of matter made up of two or more atoms joined together.

physical property (FIHZ ih kuhl PRAP ur tee) A characteristic of matter that can be measured or observed without changing matter into something new.

states of matter (stayts uhv MAT ur) The three forms that matter usually takes: solid, liquid, and gas.

volume (VAHL yoom) The amount of space that matter takes up.

weight (wayt) The measure of the pull of gravity on an object.

Think About What You Have Read

Vocabulary

❶ Weight is a measure of _____ .

A) the amount of space an object takes up

B) how fast the particles in an object move

C) the amount of matter in an object

D) the pull of gravity on an object

Comprehension

❷ What is the difference between an atom and a molecule?

❸ What units would a scientist most likely use to measure the length of a small object?

❹ What are some physical and chemical properties of paper that can be seen?

Critical Thinking

❺ Compare the mass of a person on Earth with the mass of the same person on the Moon. Then compare the weight of a person on Earth with the weight of the same person on the Moon.

How Matter Changes

Contents

What Are Physical Changes in Matter?

Physical changes are changes in size, shape, or state. Physical changes do not make new kinds of matter form. Energy is a part of all changes in matter.

Size, Shape, and State

Suppose you are playing baseball with your friends. You hit the ball and it cracks a window of your house. The glass breaks into hundreds of tiny pieces. Your baseball has caused a physical change in the window glass. A **physical change** changes the way matter looks. It does not change it into a new kind of matter.

Many physical changes change the size, shape, or state of matter. The shape and size of the window glass changed when it broke, but each piece of broken glass still had the properties of glass. No new kinds of matter were formed.

The shape and size of the candy changes when it is hit with the hammer. The other properties of the candy stay the same.

The juice bar changes from a solid to a liquid as it melts. This is a change in state. Changes in state are physical changes.

Look at the melting juice bar. The melted part looks different from the frozen part. If you tasted the melted part of the juice bar, it would taste the same as the frozen part. The melted juice bar is not a new kind of matter. It still tastes like a frozen juice bar. It has just changed from a solid to a liquid. This change in state is a physical change.

If you hit the juice bar with a hammer, how would it change? The juice bar would probably break into smaller pieces, like the candy in the picture. The smaller pieces might melt, but new kinds of matter would not be formed.

Common Physical Changes

Look at the picture below. The student has cut and drawn on the paper and shaped the clay. You know that these changes are physical changes. They are physical changes because the paper and clay have not been changed into something new.

When matter is moved or changed, energy (EHN ur jee) is at work. **Energy** is the ability to cause change. Sometimes energy must be added to matter to make it change. For example, heat must be added to ice so the ice will melt. Heat is a form of energy. Heat is added to a glue stick in a hot glue gun. The glue stick melts when heat is added.

This student has made physical changes to the clay and paper.

Sometimes matter gives off energy when it changes. If you bend a metal paper clip back and forth many times, the clip will begin to feel warmer. That is because heat energy is given off as you bend it.

Think about physical changes that happen every day. Ice melts. Glass breaks. You cut some paper. These changes in form, size, and shape need energy. Heat energy from the Sun melts the ice. The energy of a moving baseball breaks the glass. The energy in your body helps you cut out a snowflake.

CAUSE AND EFFECT

How does matter change in a physical change?

2

What Happens When Matter Is Heated or Cooled?

Heating and cooling matter changes the way its particles move and the amount of space between the particles.

Thermal Energy and Matter

Suppose you have a small box and some marbles. You fill just the bottom of the box with a tight layer of marbles. If you shake the box lightly, the marbles might move a little, but they will not move very much. They are packed too tightly together to spread out. The marbles are like particles in a solid. When the marbles move, they have just a little bit of energy of motion.

You could say that the marbles have very little thermal energy (THUR muhl EHN ur jee). **Thermal energy** is the total energy of the particles of matter. It has to do with the energy of moving particles. The particles of a solid have very little energy of motion.

Solid Iron

The particles in this piece of solid iron are packed tightly together. They have very little energy of motion.

Liquid Iron

The particles of liquid iron are farther apart than the particles of solid iron. This change of state happens because thermal energy has been added to the iron.

If you shake the box of marbles harder, you add more energy to the marbles. The marbles will move apart farther and faster. Particles of matter move like this. If you add more energy to particles of matter, they will move faster and farther apart.

Thermal energy can be added and taken away from matter. You cannot see thermal energy, but you can feel it as heat. **Heat** (heet) is the flow of thermal energy from a warmer area to a cooler area.

When you heat matter, its thermal energy grows. The particles of matter move faster and farther apart. When you cool matter, you take away thermal energy. The particles of matter slow down and move closer together.

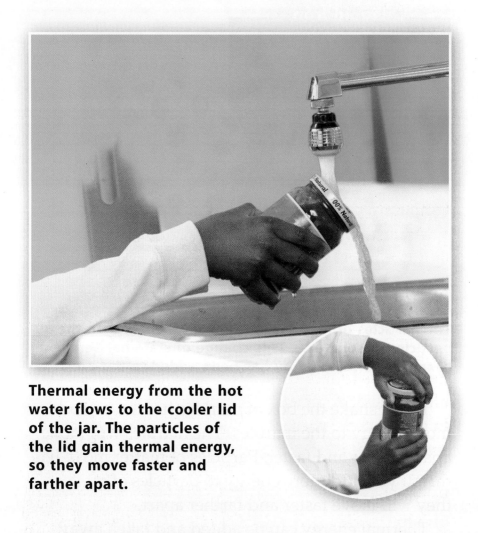

Thermal energy from the hot water flows to the cooler lid of the jar. The particles of the lid gain thermal energy, so they move faster and farther apart.

Look at the picture above. Have you ever tried to open a jar with a tight lid? If you heat a metal jar lid with hot water, its particles move faster and farther apart. The lid gets larger, or expands, and loosens from the jar. If you cooled the lid, it would cause the particles to move more slowly and get closer together. The lid would get tighter, or contract, on the jar.

Temperature

On a snowy day, the air outside is much colder than the air inside your house. You can find out how much colder by measuring the air temperature (TEHM pur uh chur). **Temperature** is used to measure how hot or cold matter is. Temperature also tells how fast the particles of matter are moving. Particles of matter move more slowly in cold temperatures and faster in warm temperatures.

A thermometer (thur MAHM-ih tur) is a tool that measures temperature. Thermometers measure temperature in units called degrees. Scientists and people in some countries use the Celsius (SEHL see-uhs) scale of degrees. In the United States, temperature is measured using the Fahrenheit (FAR-uhn hyt) scale.

You can read a thermometer to know how warmly to dress.

This picture was taken with a special camera that makes heat look red in the picture. It shows that thermal energy is moving from warm parts of the house to the cooler outside air. The outside air gets warmer as the inside air gets cooler.

When you add heat to an object, its temperature will go up. As you cook, you add heat to food. The heat goes into the food. The food gets warmer and has a higher temperature.

How can you lower the temperature of an object? Remember that heat is the flow of thermal energy from a warmer place to a cooler place. To lower the temperature of an object, you must put it in a cooler place, such as a refrigerator or freezer. Heat will move out of the warmer object into the colder air inside the refrigerator or freezer.

Changes in State

The temperature of matter makes it a solid, liquid, or gas. When matter is heated or cooled, its temperature changes, and it changes state. Melting, freezing, boiling, and condensation are physical changes in the state of matter.

When heat is added to matter, the particles of matter move faster and farther apart. Particles in a solid are held in place close together. When you heat a solid, its particles move faster and faster until they break out of their places. This change in state is melting—a solid becoming a liquid.

Over time, parts of this floating piece of ice will melt. When ice melts, water changes from a solid to a liquid. This is a physical change.

Particles in a liquid can move past each other, but they stay close together. When you heat a liquid, its particles move faster and faster until they spread even farther apart. The liquid becomes a gas during a change in state called evaporation. Particles in a gas move quickly and there is much space between them. At very high temperatures, liquid evaporates quickly. Boiling is very fast evaporation.

Change the State

Starting State of Matter		Change	Ending State of Matter	
Solid		**Melting** Adding thermal energy to turn a solid into a liquid	Liquid	
Liquid		**Freezing** Taking away thermal energy to turn a liquid into a solid	Solid	
Liquid		**Boiling** Adding thermal energy to turn a liquid into a gas	Gas	
Gas		**Condensation** Taking away thermal energy so a gas or vapor cools and turns into a liquid	Liquid	

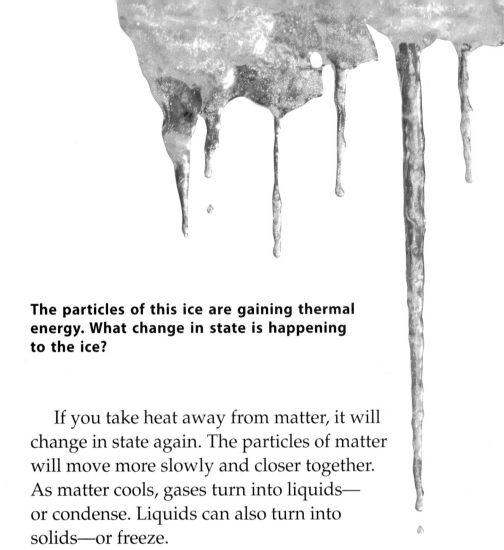

The particles of this ice are gaining thermal energy. What change in state is happening to the ice?

If you take heat away from matter, it will change in state again. The particles of matter will move more slowly and closer together. As matter cools, gases turn into liquids— or condense. Liquids can also turn into solids—or freeze.

Changes in state are physical changes. The matter looks different, but it is not a new kind of matter. In changes of state, the matter looks different because the particles of matter are in different places. The particles have not changed. The particles of ice are the same as the particles of liquid water. They are just packed together in different ways.

Particles that are held together more strongly, such as in solids, need more energy to break them apart.

Matter Stays the Same

Matter might look different after a physical change, but the kind of matter itself does not change. Its particles have not changed. They are just packed together differently.

After a physical change, the matter's physical properties, such as color and density, stay the same. Its mass, or amount of matter, also stays the same. For example, when 100 g (3.5 oz) of ice melt, the mass of liquid water that forms will also be 100 g.

This man is using thermal energy to make iron soft.

Water is not the only kind of matter that changes state. Metals, such as iron, can also change state. When iron is heated, it gets soft. Soft metals can be hammered and bent into different shapes. When you add more heat, the metal gets softer and softer. Finally, it melts into a liquid. It has changed state, but its physical properties are still the same. It is not a new kind of matter.

Look at the pictures. The man is changing hot, soft iron into different shapes. The iron cools and hardens into its new shape—a gate.

CLASSIFY

Classify each of the following changes according to whether they are caused by adding heat or taking heat away: boiling, condensation, melting, freezing.

3 What Are Mixtures and Solutions?

Mixtures and solutions are made up of two or more things—or substances—that are put together during a physical change.

Mixtures

What is at the bottom of your backpack? It could be pencils, paper clips, and papers mixed together, or combined. This combination of things is a mixture (MIHKS chur). A **mixture** is matter made up of two or more substances that are combined.

Making a mixture is a physical change. The pencils, paper clips, and papers are all mixed up, but their physical properties have not changed. The pencils are still pencils.

It would be easy to separate the substances, or sort them into groups, by looking at their different physical properties. When substances in a mixture are very different, it is easier to separate them. Separating the parts of a mixture is a physical change.

This mixture of tiny pieces of iron and sand is easy to separate by using a magnet.

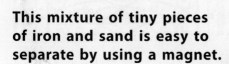

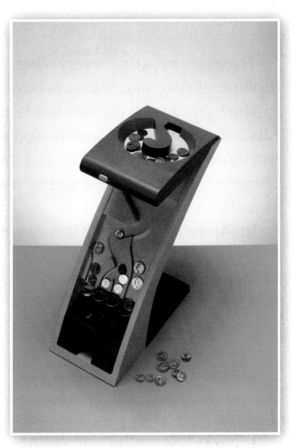

This machine can separate a mixture of coins into groups of coins with the same size.

You cannot separate all mixtures by hand. Some mixtures can be separated using a change in state. To separate a mixture of sugar and water, you could boil it. The water would change to a gas, or evaporate, and only the sugar would be left.

Different densities can also be used to separate a mixture. Density is a physical property of matter, like mass and volume. Soil could be separated into its parts by mixing it with water and letting the mixture rest. The most dense soil parts, like stones, would sink first. The less dense soil parts, like sand or clay, would sink later.

Some Common Mixtures

There are mixtures everywhere. Bubbles are a mixture of soap and water. A bowl of soup is a mixture. Your sock drawer holds a mixture of socks. Mixtures can be any combination of matter. Some mixtures are solids, liquids, and gases together. Other mixtures have just solids, just liquids, or just gases.

In mixtures like soup, it is easy to see the separate parts. You can see carrots in some places and noodles in other places. You can see that the substances in soup still have their physical properties.

In other mixtures, you cannot see the separate parts. In lemonade, you cannot see the water, lemon juice, and sugar that make up the mixture. These separate parts cannot be seen, but they still have their own physical properties.

You cannot see the separate substances, but these bubbles are a mixture of soap and water.

Look for mixtures in the picture below. Some mixtures are easier to see than others. Fog is a mixture of air and water. Air is a mixture of gases. Sea water is a mixture of water and salts. The lighthouse is made of many different mixtures. Concrete is a mixture. The glass and metal parts are mixtures. Even the paint on the lighthouse is a mixture.

Fog is a mixture of air and water.
Air is a mixture of gases.

Solutions

A mixture of sand and water looks different from a mixture of salt and water. You can see the particles of sand in the first mixture. You cannot see the particles of salt in the second mixture. If you taste it, you know the salt is still there.

Salt water is a mixture called a solution (suh LOO shun). In a **solution**, the particles of one kind of matter are mixed evenly with the particles of other kinds of matter. The whole solution has the same properties.

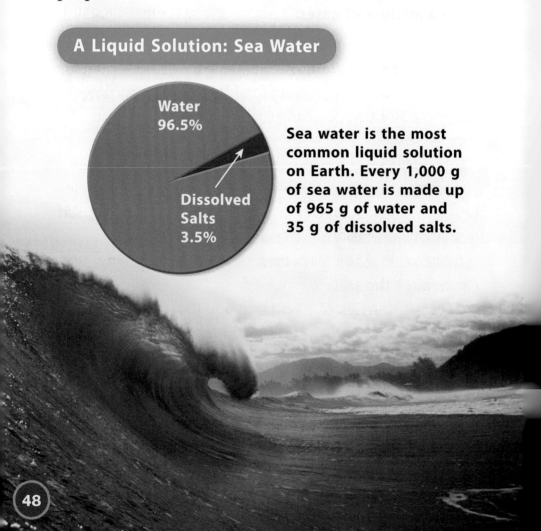

A Liquid Solution: Sea Water

Water 96.5%

Dissolved Salts 3.5%

Sea water is the most common liquid solution on Earth. Every 1,000 g of sea water is made up of 965 g of water and 35 g of dissolved salts.

You are looking at salt under a microscope!

You cannot see the salt in salt water because it has dissolved. To **dissolve** (dih ZAHLV) means to mix completely by separating into particles that you cannot see.

As salt dissolves in water, the particles of water circle around the particles of salt. The water particles and salt particles move together. After time, the solid salt is broken down into particles that are mixed evenly with water particles. When this happens, you cannot see the salt.

The properties of a solution are often different from the properties of its separate parts, but dissolving is a physical change. The physical properties of the parts of the solution stay the same.

A solution can be separated back into its parts, but not by hand. When the water evaporates from a salt water solution, the salt is left behind.

Sand is not soluble in water. No particles of sand are dissolved in this beaker of water.

Salt is more soluble in water than sand. Some salt has sunk to the bottom of the beaker.

Sugar is very soluble in water. All of the sugar has dissolved in the water.

Comparing Solutions

Look at the mixtures in the glass beakers. The same amount of solid was added to equal amounts of water in each one. Some solids dissolve in water better than others. Solubility (sahl yuh BIHL ih tee) is a measure of how much of a substance can dissolve in another substance. The solubility of a substance changes in different temperatures and different substances.

Look again at the three beakers. If you add sand to a beaker of water, all of the sand will sink to the bottom of the beaker. Sand is not soluble in water. Sand particles cannot separate and mix with water particles.

Salt and sugar are both soluble in water at room temperature. You can see that sugar is more soluble than salt.

Because solutions are mixtures, it does not matter exactly how much of each part is mixed together. A solution of salt water can have a lot of salt and taste very salty. Or, it can have only a little salt and taste only a little salty. Both mixtures are solutions of salt water.

TEXT STRUCTURE

Where in the text of this lesson would you find examples of common mixtures?

4 | What Are Chemical Changes in Matter?

A chemical change makes new kinds of matter.

New Matter

Do you like waffles? Waffles are made using a mixture of flour, sugar, oil, and eggs. Can you taste the eggs in waffles? Not really. As you cook the waffles, the properties of the flour, sugar, oil, and eggs change. That is why you cannot taste the eggs. Cooking the waffles is not a physical change. It is a chemical change.

A **chemical change** is a change in matter that makes new kinds of matter with different properties. A chemical change needs energy. Energy is given off or taken in during a chemical change. When you make waffles, the flour, sugar, oil, and eggs take in energy to form a new kind of matter—a waffle!

Cooking is a chemical change that changes the parts of waffle batter into new matter—the waffles.

A burning fire is a chemical change that gives off heat and light, which are two kinds of energy.

Particles of matter—atoms and molecules—are part of physical changes and chemical changes. During a physical change, atoms and molecules move. During a chemical change, molecules break apart and mix in different ways with other atoms and molecules. This forms new matter with different properties. The atoms and molecules mix in new ways during a chemical reaction (ree AK shuhn). A **chemical reaction** is a chemical change.

In a chemical reaction, the matter that you start with is called the **reactant** (ree AK tuhnt). When you make waffles, the reactants are flour, sugar, oil, and eggs. The **product** of a chemical reaction is the new matter that forms. Waffles are the product when you cook the waffle batter.

Common Chemical Changes

Chemical changes are everywhere. Cars burn gas in a chemical reaction that makes energy to move the car. Burning wood and rusting metal are also chemical changes. Your body uses chemical reactions to change food into the molecules and energy you need to grow.

Thermal energy is the kind of energy most often found during chemical changes. It can be added or taken away. Light, electricity, sound, and motion are other kinds of energy that can be found during chemical changes.

Bubbles and changes in color, state, temperature, smell, and energy tell you that a chemical change is happening. The biggest sign of a chemical change is that new products form that have properties that are different from those of the reactants.

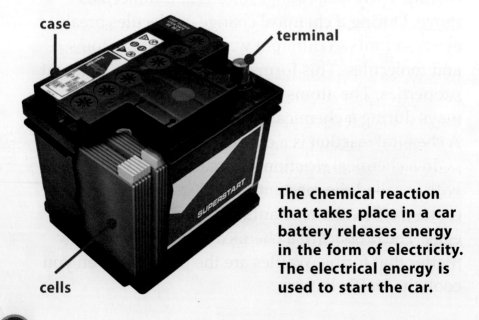

case

terminal

cells

The chemical reaction that takes place in a car battery releases energy in the form of electricity. The electrical energy is used to start the car.

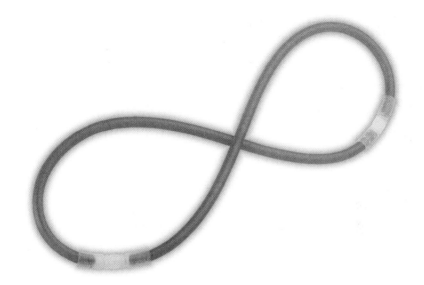

Two reactants are mixed together inside a glow stick. This makes a chemical reaction that makes the liquid inside the stick light up—or glow.

How does a chemical change take place? Atoms and molecules are held together by forces called chemical bonds. During a chemical reaction, the chemical bonds are broken. New bonds form between different atoms and molecules. This causes new matter, or products, to form. The new products are made up of different atoms and molecules, so they have different properties from the reactants.

Energy is often given off during a chemical reaction. This energy can warm a house, start a car, or light up a dark room. Sometimes the energy that is given off can be dangerous. The energy can make something blow up. This can wreck buildings and hurt people.

Comparing Physical and Chemical Changes

You have learned about physical and chemical changes in matter. In a physical change, no new matter is formed. The matter might look different, but the chemical bonds between the particles of matter have not been broken. A pool of water that freezes into solid ice goes through a physical change.

In a chemical change, a new kind of matter always forms. The new matter looks different and has different physical properties. This is because the chemical bonds between the particles of the reactants have been broken. New bonds have formed. A piece of wood that burns into ash goes through a chemical change.

A Chemical Reaction: Medicine in Water

BUBBLES As the medicine dissolves in the water, a chemical reaction happens.

LIQUID

MEDICINE

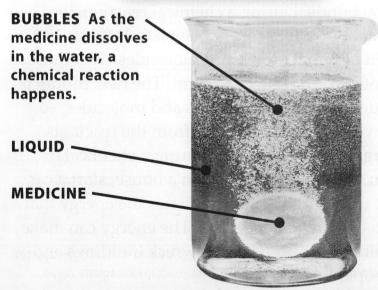

Bubbles tell you that a chemical reaction is taking place.

Comparing Changes in Matter

Physical Changes	Chemical Changes

Crushing a sugar cube does not change the kind of matter. Tiny pieces of sugar are still sugar.	Sticky caramel is sugar that has been burned. Heat changes the sugar particles into new matter—caramel.

Folding paper does not break chemical bonds. No new bonds are formed. Folded paper is still paper.	When paper is burned, it turns to ash.

It is easy to bend copper. Bending a copper tube does not break chemical bonds. Copper is still copper.	Water in the air mixes with the copper in this penny to form a green coating.

Have you ever cooked a marshmallow over a fire? Cooking a marshmallow can make it warm and soft or brown and hard. It takes more time and more heat from the fire—more energy—to make a marshmallow brown and hard. Marshmallows that are brown and hard have had a chemical change. Chemical changes often need more energy than physical changes.

It also takes energy to separate physical and chemical combinations. Physical combinations are mixtures like sugar water. Chemical combinations, or chemical compounds, are combinations of atoms that are held together by chemical bonds. Sugar is a chemical compound. It takes different kinds and amounts of energy to separate physical and chemical combinations.

CAUSE AND EFFECT

What happens when new chemical bonds are formed?

Glossary

chemical change (KEHM ih kuhl chaynj) A change in matter that produces new kinds of matter with different properties.

chemical reaction (KEHM ih kuhl ree AK shuhn) Another term for a chemical change.

dissolve (dih ZAHLV) To mix completely with another substance to form a solution.

energy (EHN ur jee) The ability to cause change.

heat (heet) The flow of thermal energy from a warmer area to a cooler area.

mixture (MIHKS chur) Matter made up of two or more substances or materials that are physically combined.

Glossary

physical change (FIHZ ih kuhl chaynj) A change in the size, shape, or state of matter that does not change it into a new kind of matter.

product (PRAHD uhkt) The newly formed matter in a chemical reaction.

reactant (ree AK tuhnt) The matter that you start with in a chemical reaction.

solution (suh LOO shuhn) A mixture in which the particles of one kind of matter are mixed evenly with the particles of other kinds of matter.

temperature (TEHM pur uh chur) A measure of how hot or cold matter is.

thermal energy (THUR muhl EHN ur jee) The total kinetic energy of tiny moving particles of matter.

Think About What You Have Read

Vocabulary

❶ During a chemical change, _____ are broken and reformed.

A) molecules

B) forms of energy

C) reactants

D) products

Comprehension

❷ How does heating affect particles of matter?

❸ What is a solution? Give an example of a solution.

❹ How are new kinds of matter formed in a chemical change?

Critical Thinking

❺ A friend tells you that baked cookies are exactly the same matter as the dough used to make them. Discuss this idea and explain whether you think it is true or false.

Energy Changes

Contents

How Does Energy Change Form?

Energy has different forms. One form of energy can change to another form.

Potential and Kinetic Energy

Energy is being able to move or make something change. Often you can see energy as motion. Sometimes you cannot see energy, because it is stored in an object. The diver standing on the diving platform is not moving. She does not seem to have any energy.

But the diver has stored energy. When she dives, you can see the energy as movement. This energy is not created. It has just changed from stored energy to energy of motion. **Potential energy** (puh TEHN shul EHN ur jee) is energy that is stored in an object. It is energy that can cause motion or some other change.

You cannot see the potential energy stored in the diver waiting to dive.

You can see kinetic energy in motion when the diver dives into the pool.

The diver on the platform has potential energy. It changes to energy of motion when she dives. A fuel such as gasoline has potential energy. It burns and produces motion in the engine of a car.

The energy that an object has when it is moving is **kinetic energy** (kuh NEHT ihk EHN ur jee). Energy often changes back and forth between potential and kinetic energy. When the diver moves and dives into the water, potential energy becomes kinetic energy. When the diver goes back up on the platform and stands still again, kinetic energy becomes potential energy.

Forms of Energy

Energy can take many different forms. Electrical energy is a form of energy that you can use to run some machines. Light energy is a form of energy that you can see. Sound energy is a form of energy that you can hear. Thermal energy is a form of energy that you can feel as heat. Mechanical energy is a form of energy an object in motion has. Chemical energy is a form of energy stored in matter.

Energy can change from one form to another. This change is called energy transformation (trans fur MAY shun). The pictures show an example of energy transformation.

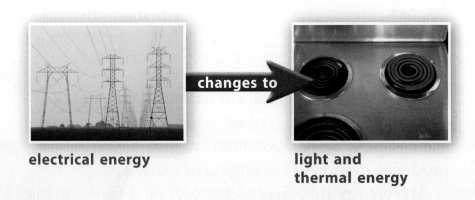

electrical energy   changes to   light and thermal energy

COMPARE AND CONTRAST

How do potential energy and kinetic energy differ?

2   How Does Light Behave?

Light moves in waves. Moving waves of light can bounce and bend. Light waves go into some objects and pass through others.

Properties of Light

Light is a form of energy that you can see when it interacts with matter. Light travels in waves. Waves carry energy. The picture shows what a wave looks like. A high point of a wave is called a crest. A low point is called a trough (trawf). Halfway between a crest and a trough is the resting point. A wave has length and height. The length of a wave is its wavelength. The height of a wave is its amplitude (AM plih tood).

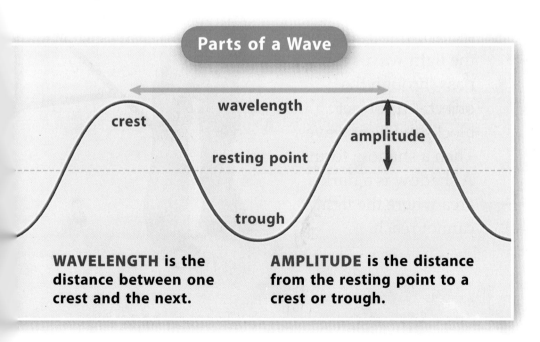

Parts of a Wave

crest

wavelength

amplitude

resting point

trough

WAVELENGTH is the distance between one crest and the next.

AMPLITUDE is the distance from the resting point to a crest or trough.

You have probably seen waves in water. If you drop a pebble in the water, water waves spread out in all directions. Like water waves, light waves move in all directions from a light source. A light source may be a light bulb, a fire, or the Sun. Light waves can move through matter, air, or space. Light from the Sun travels millions of kilometers through space to reach Earth. Most objects that give off light also give off heat.

Light waves keep traveling in a straight line until they hit something. Sometimes the light waves cannot pass through the object. The object blocks the light waves. Then a shadow forms. A shadow is a dark area where the light cannot reach.

The girl blocks some of the light waves, making a shadow.

Most of the light waves that hit smooth water bounce off the surface. This is called reflection.

Behavior of Light

When light waves hit an object, the waves can behave in four different ways. The waves can be reflected, transmitted, refracted, or absorbed. How light waves behave depends on the properties of the object they hit.

Reflection (rih FLEHK shuhn) is what happens when light waves hit a surface and bounce off. When you see an object, you are really seeing light bouncing off the object. For example, you can see this page because it reflects some light into your eyes.

Most surfaces reflect at least some of the light that hits them. Smooth surfaces, such as a mirror, reflect almost all the light that hits them. This makes the surface look shiny.

The pencil in the glass of water looks broken because of refraction.

Some materials transmit most of the light that hits them. This means the light waves pass through the materials. However, these materials may cause light to slow down and bend. The bending of light waves is called **refraction** (rih FRAHK shuhn). Refraction can make objects look as though they are bent or broken. Glass, water, and clear plastic can transmit and refract light.

Some materials take in, or absorb (uhb SAWRB), most of the light that hits them. You cannot see light that is absorbed, because it is not reflected back to your eyes. When light waves are absorbed, the light energy changes into thermal energy, or heat. That is why objects in sunlight get hot.

Dark-colored objects absorb more light than light-colored objects. A black shirt absorbs more light than a white shirt. The light absorbed by the black shirt changes into thermal energy.

A prism separates white light into colors. Raindrops act like tiny prisms to form a rainbow.

Colors of Light

The color of light depends on its wavelength. Red light has the longest wavelength. Then comes orange, yellow, green, and blue light. Violet has the shortest. Light that is made up of all colors is called white light. Sunlight is white light.

A prism (PRIHZ uhm) is an object that refracts, or bends, light. A prism separates white light into all its different colors.

The color of an object depends on the color of light that it reflects. For example, a green object reflects green light. It absorbs most other colors of light.

MAIN IDEA AND DETAILS

What is refraction?

How Does Sound Behave?

Sound is a form of energy that you can hear. Sound moves in waves that are made by vibrations.

How Sounds Are Made

Sound is a form of energy made by vibrations (vy BRAY shuhnz). A **vibration** is a back-and-forth motion of very small pieces of matter called particles. Stretch a rubber band between your fingers. Then pull on the rubber band and let it go. It will move back and forth quickly. You can see and hear and feel it vibrating. Sometimes if music is playing very loud, you can feel the vibrations as well as hear the sound.

When a material vibrates, it creates sound waves. As a sound wave moves through matter, particles are pushed together. Then the particles spread apart.

A spring moves back and forth when it is pushed together and then let go. Sound waves move in the same way.

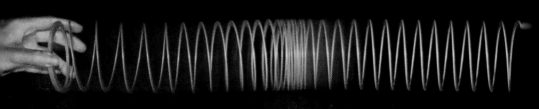

The strings of this bass vibrate when a bow is moved across them.

At first, air particles bunch together in a sound wave.

Then air particles spread apart in a sound wave.

All sounds are made by vibrations of matter. Look at the picture. When the girl moves a bow across the strings, the strings vibrate. The vibrating strings cause sound waves to move through the air. First the air particles bunch together. Then the particles spread apart as the sound waves move away.

Put your hand on your throat as you sing or speak. You can feel vibrations in your throat. These vibrations cause sound waves that are the sound of your voice.

Properties of Sound

Sound waves are like light waves in that they have wavelength and amplitude. In a sound wave, wavelength is the distance between where particles are bunched together and where particles are spread apart.

Amplitude is a measure of how close or far apart the particles are. As a sound wave moves through a material, it bunches up, spreads apart, bunches up, and spreads apart again and again.

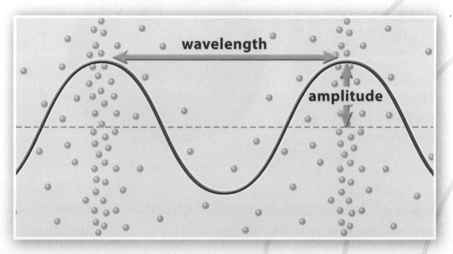

Sound waves have wavelength and amplitude. Particles are bunched together at the high points of the wave. Particles are spread apart at the low points.

The greater the amplitude of a sound wave, the more energy it has. A sound wave that has more energy sounds louder. The loudness of a sound is called **volume**. Volume depends on the amplitude of a sound wave.

Volume also depends on how far the listener is from what is making the sound. This is because the amount of energy in sound waves spreads out as the waves move farther away.

Also like light waves, sound waves move away from a source in all directions. Sound waves can travel through air, water, and many solid materials. However, sound waves cannot move through empty space. Sound waves must have some type of material to move through.

The sound of the vibrating cymbal spreads out from the cymbal in all directions.

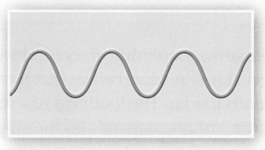

This sound wave has a low frequency and a low pitch.

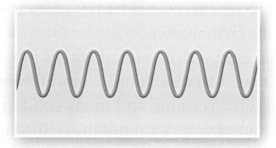

This sound wave has a higher frequency and a higher pitch than the sound wave above.

Frequency (FREE kwuhn see) is another property of sound waves. Frequency is the number of crests and troughs produced in a certain amount of time, such as a second. The frequency of sound waves determines the pitch (pitch) of the sound. Pitch is how high or low a sound seems to a listener.

Sounds with a low frequency produce a low number of crests and troughs in a second. Sounds with a low frequency also have a low pitch. Sounds with a high frequency produce many crests and troughs in a second. Sounds with a high frequency also have a high pitch.

How You Hear Sound

People hear sound with their ears. The outer ear gathers sound waves. The sound waves are passed into the ear. Inside is a flap of skin called the eardrum. The eardrum vibrates when sound waves hit it. The eardrum passes the vibrations to the middle ear.

The middle ear passes the vibrations to the inner ear. In the inner ear, the vibrations cause nerve cells to send signals to the brain. The brain reads the signals as sound.

Some animals have ears that are more sensitive to sound than people are. For example, dogs can hear sounds that people can't.

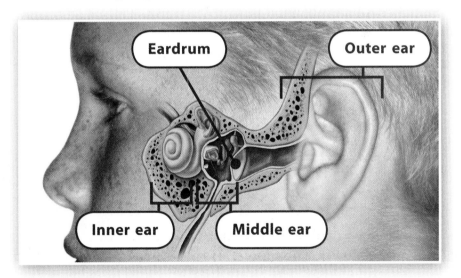

Eardrum

Outer ear

Inner ear

Middle ear

CAUSE AND EFFECT

What two things affect the loudness of a sound?

4 What Is Thermal Energy?

Thermal energy is the kinetic energy of movement of tiny particles of matter. Thermal energy can move from one form of matter to another as heat.

Thermal Energy and Temperature

All matter is made up of tiny particles. These particles are always moving and producing kinetic energy. The kinetic energy of moving particles is called **thermal** (THUR muhl) **energy**.

Thermal energy produces heat. **Heat** is a measure of the movement of thermal energy from one form of matter to another. Thermal energy moves between warm and cool matter. Hot cocoa has so much thermal energy it is too hot to drink. But after some time in the cold air, the particles in the cocoa slow down. Some of the heat in the cocoa moves into the cold air. The cocoa loses some of its thermal energy. It becomes cool enough to sip.

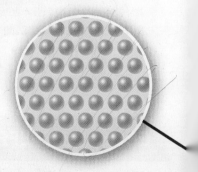

Particles of the cold skate blade move slowly. They have less kinetic energy. The skate blade has a low temperature.

The picture shows how kinetic energy can be different in different objects. Something hot has a different amount of kinetic energy than something cold. The particles in the cocoa are moving fast. They have high kinetic energy. The particles in the skate blade are moving more slowly. They have less kinetic energy.

Temperature (TEHM pur uh chur) describes the average kinetic energy of particles in matter. The more kinetic energy particles have, the higher their temperature. The particles in hot cocoa have high kinetic energy. Hot cocoa has a high temperature. The particles in a cold skate blade have low kinetic energy. The skate blade has a low temperature.

Particles of hot cocoa move quickly. They have a lot of kinetic energy. The cocoa has a high temperature.

Transfer of Thermal Energy

Thermal energy can be transferred from warmer matter to cooler matter. You saw how thermal energy moves from hot cocoa to cooler air. Heat moves between particles of matter that touch each other. Particles in hot cocoa touch particles in cooler air. Thermal energy moves from the cocoa into the air. That makes the cocoa feel cooler.

When you touch something with your hand, it either feels cool or warm. This depends on how thermal energy is being transferred. When thermal energy moves from matter to your hand, the matter feels warm to you. When thermal energy moves from your hand to matter, the matter feels cool to you. Thermal energy can be transferred from warm matter to cooler matter in two ways.

Thermal energy from a fire can transfer to particles of air. The air particles bump into your cool hands. The air feels warm to you.

Conduction Two kinds of matter often touch each other. The transfer of thermal energy between particles of matter that are touching is called **conduction** (kuhn DUHK shuhn). It occurs mainly in solids. Conduction happens when fast-moving particles bump into nearby slow-moving particles. The fast-moving particles give some of their kinetic energy to the slower particles.

Look at the picture of the stove. Fast-moving particles of the hot stove burner bump into slow-moving particles of the cool frying pan. The particles of the pan get more kinetic energy and move faster. They heat up. When the pan gets hot, conduction transfers thermal energy to the food in the pan. The food heats up.

Thermal energy can move from the burner to the pan. It can also move from the pan to the food. This is called conduction.

Convection Thermal energy can also be transferred through fluids (FLOO ihdz). Fluids are liquids and gases, such as water and air. **Convection** (kuhn VEHK shuhn) is the transfer of thermal energy through fluids.

Convection occurs because the density of different fluids is different. Density is the amount of matter in a given space. Particles of warm fluids have more kinetic energy and are farther apart than particles in cool fluids.

The heater on the floor warms the air it touches. The warm air moves around the room on a convection current.

Since particles of warm fluids are farther apart, warm fluids are less dense than cool fluids. As a result, warm fluids usually rise, and cool fluids usually sink.

In the picture, air on one side of the room is warmed by the heater. The warm air rises because it is less dense than the cool air. Cool air sinks to take the place of the warm air. This goes on until all the air is heated. This flow of air is called a convection current.

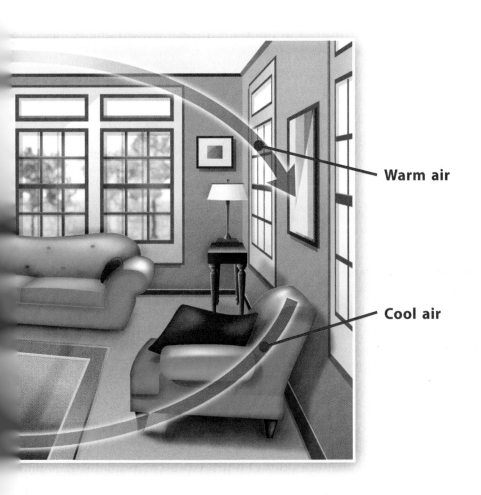

Warm air

Cool air

Radiation

Most objects that give off light also give off heat. Like light from the Sun, heat from the Sun travels in waves through space as radiant energy. Radiant energy is also given off by other sources of heat, such as heat lamps and fires.

When radiant energy hits matter, it changes into thermal energy. This transfer of heat by waves is called **radiation** (ray dee AY shuhn). Matter absorbs radiant energy. When you absorb radiant energy, you feel the heat when it changes into thermal energy.

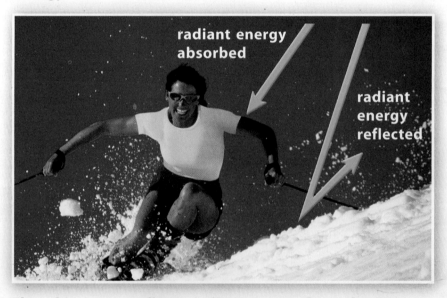

radiant energy absorbed

radiant energy reflected

The white snow reflects radiant energy from the Sun.

DRAW CONCLUSIONS

How does heat travel when you cook vegetables in a hot frying pan?

Glossary

conduction (kuhn DUHK shuhn) The transfer of thermal energy from particle to particle between two objects that are touching.

convection (kuhn VEHK shuhn) The transfer of thermal energy by the movement of fluids.

heat (heet) 1. The flow of thermal energy from a warmer area to a cooler area; 2. a measure of how much thermal energy is transferred from one substance to another.

kinetic energy (kuh NEHT ihk EHN ur jee) The energy that an object has because it is moving.

light (lyt) A form of energy that travels in waves and can be seen when it interacts with matter.

potential energy (puh TEHN shuhl EHN ur jee) The energy that is stored in an object.

radiation (ray dee AY shuhn) The transfer of energy by waves.

reflection (rih FLEHK shuhn) What occurs when light waves bounce off a surface.

refraction (rih FRAK shuhn) What occurs when light waves bend as they pass from one material to another.

sound (sownd) A form of energy that is produced by vibrations and can be heard.

temperature (TEHM pur uh chur) 1. A measure of how hot or cold matter is; 2. the average kinetic energy of the particles of a substance.

thermal energy (THUR muhl EHN ur jee) The total kinetic energy of tiny moving particles of matter.

vibration (vy BRAY shuhn) A back-and-forth movement of matter.

volume (VAHL yoom) 1. The amount of space that matter takes up; 2. The loudness of a sound.

Think About What You Have Read

Vocabulary

❶ The transfer of thermal energy by the movement of fluids is called _____ .

A) absorption

B) convection

C) conduction

D) radiation

Comprehension

❷ What are four ways that light waves can behave when they hit an object?

❸ How is sound produced?

❹ What is thermal energy?

Critical Thinking

❺ Which shirt would help drivers see you at night: a shirt that absorbs light or a shirt that reflects light? Explain.

Electricity and Magnetism

Contents

What Is Static Electricity?

ELECTRICALLY NEUTRAL
Matter that has the same number of positive and negative charges

All matter is made up of tiny particles. Some have a positive electric charge. Some have a negative charge.

Electric Charges

Have you ever felt a shock from a doorknob after walking on a carpet? Here's why. You know that all matter is made up of tiny particles called atoms. Doorknobs and carpet are made of atoms. Atoms are made up of even tinier particles. Many of these tiny particles carry units of electricity called **electric charges**. These charges gave you the shock.

There are positive ⊕ electric charges and negative ⊖ electric charges. Charges that are the same are called like charges. Charges that are different are called unlike charges. Most matter is electrically neutral. Electrically neutral means matter has an equal number of positive and negative charges.

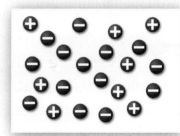

NEGATIVELY CHARGED
Matter that has more negative than positive charges

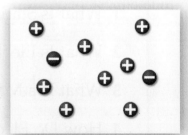

POSITIVELY CHARGED
Matter that has more positive than negative charges

How Charges Behave

Electric charges can act on each other, even without touching. Like charges repel. They push away from each other. Unlike charges attract. They pull toward each other. Two objects with like charges push away from each other. Two objects with unlike charges pull toward each other.

Negative charges are attracted to positive charges. Particles that have a negative charge can move more easily from one material to another than particles with a positive charge can. So negative charges tend to move toward matter that is positively charged.

Negative charges do not usually move toward an electrically neutral object. However, negative charges can be made to move. Rubbing can move negative charges from one electrically neutral object to another.

Rubbing a balloon with a wool cloth causes negative charges to move from the cloth to the balloon.

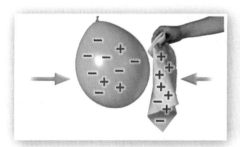 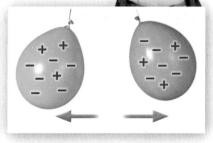

UNLIKE CHARGES ATTRACT
When brought close together, objects with unlike charges attract each other.

LIKE CHARGES REPEL
When brought close together, objects with like charges repel each other.

Buildup and Discharge

Sometimes an electric charge builds up on a material. This built-up electric charge is called **static electricity** (STAT ihk ih lehk TRIHS ih tee). When your hair stands on end and moves toward a plastic comb, you can see static electricity at work.

Running a comb through your hair moves negatively charged particles from your hair onto the comb. Your hair loses negative charges and has an overall positive charge. The comb gains negative charges and now has an overall negative charge.

Your hair and the comb now have unlike charges. They attract each other. Each hair on your head now has a like charge. They repel each other. The result is they stand on end and push away from each other.

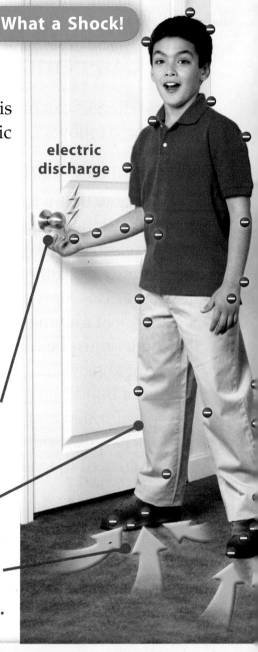

You sometimes get a shock when you touch a metal doorknob. The shock is caused by a release of electric charges. In the picture, the boy's body has built up a negative charge. When he touches the doorknob, the charge quickly jumps from him to the doorknob. This release of the built-up negative charge is called an electric discharge, or spark.

electric discharge

❸ **Shock! The boy reaches for the metal doorknob. There is a discharge of static electricity.**

❷ **The boy's body becomes negatively charged.**

❶ **Rubbing against the carpet causes negative charges to build up on the boy's shoes.**

CAUSE AND EFFECT

How do like charges act on each other? How do unlike charges act on each other?

2

What Is Electric Current?

Electric charges can move if they have a complete pathway to follow.

How Charges Move

You know that when charged particles build up on matter, static electricity is produced. The charges in static electricity might stay in place. Or they might jump to another material in a sudden electric discharge. This kind of energy is not very useful. For the energy of moving charged particles to be useful, the energy must be controlled.

Charged particles can be made to move, or flow, instead of building up. The energy of these particles can be controlled and used. The constant flow of electric charges is called **electric current**. You can use electric current to toast a piece of bread.

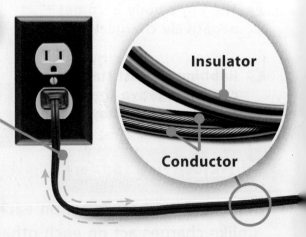

Toasting Bread

❶ When the toaster is turned on, electric charges flow out of the outlet. The charges move through one copper wire in the cord to heating coils in the toaster.

Insulator

Conductor

Conductors and Insulators

Negatively charged particles move easily through materials called **conductors** (kuhn DUHK tuhrz). Electric current easily passes through some metals. Metals such as copper and silver are good conductors. Water and living things are also good conductors.

Materials that electric charges do not flow through easily are called **insulators** (IHN suh lay tuhrz). Materials such as plastic and rubber are good insulators. Conductors and insulators are used to control and direct electric flow.

A power cord has conductors and insulators. A power cord controls and directs the flow of electric current. A power cord usually has metal conductors. These wires carry electric current. They are inside a rubber or plastic insulator. The insulator keeps the electric current from escaping.

2 Charges move through the heating coils and cause them to get hot. The heated coils toast the bread.

3 Charges return to the outlet through the other wire.

Circuits and Switches

The pathway that electric current follows is called an **electric circuit** (ih LEHK trihk SUR kiht). A circuit is a closed pathway. A closed pathway does not have any gaps, or openings. Another name for a closed pathway is a complete pathway.

You can make a simple circuit. You just need wire, a battery, and a light bulb. When you connect these items without gaps, you create a closed circuit. When charges flow through the closed circuit, the light bulb will light.

If there is a gap, or opening, in the circuit, it is an open circuit. A circuit with gaps is also known as an incomplete circuit. When a circuit has gaps, electric charges cannot complete the path. The light bulb will not light.

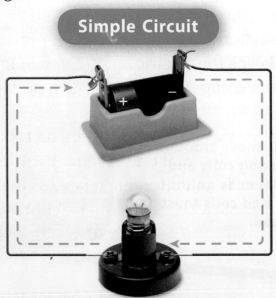

Simple Circuit

When parts of a circuit connect with no openings, the bulb lights.

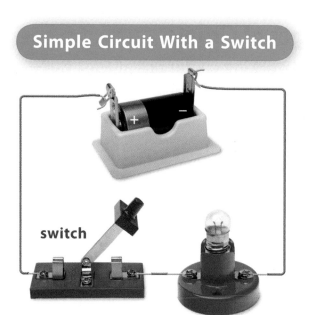

Simple Circuit With a Switch

switch

A switch is used to open and close a circuit without disconnecting the wires.

Most circuits have a switch that opens and closes the circuit. A switch lets you turn a light bulb on and off. When you flip the switch on, you close the circuit. The light bulb goes on. When you flip the switch off, you open the circuit. The light bulb goes off.

Some electrical objects are run by batteries. A battery is made up of one or more electric cells. An **electric cell** is an object that changes chemical energy into electrical energy. A flashlight is battery-powered. It is also an example of a simple circuit with a switch.

Two Types of Circuits

Every working circuit has at least three parts:
- A power source, such as a battery
- A conductor, usually wire
- An object that uses electric current, such as a light bulb.

But a circuit can have many parts. It can have a switch. It can have more than one object using the electric current.

In a **series circuit**, the parts are connected in just one pathway. Electric current flows through each part. Electric current will flow through a series circuit only if all the parts are connected.

In a **parallel circuit**, the parts are connected in more than one pathway. Electric current can flow through all the parts in many ways. Electric current will flow through a parallel circuit even if all the parts are not connected.

Circuit Pathways

SERIES CIRCUIT
If you take one part out, it makes a gap. Electric current cannot move through any of the parts.

PARALLEL CIRCUIT
If you take one part out, electric current can still move through the other parts.

This house uses parallel circuits. The circuit for the kitchen is broken, but current can still pass to the other rooms.

Electricity in the Home

The electric wiring in a house is connected in parallel circuits. If the circuit for one room is broken, electric current can still go to the circuits in the other rooms. The circuits are connected to a main source of electric current in a circuit box.

If too much electric current flows through a circuit, the wires can get too hot. Home circuits have a way to keep the house safe. In the circuit box are circuit breakers. A circuit breaker is a switch. If the circuit gets too hot, the switch opens and breaks the circuit.

COMPARE AND CONTRAST

What is the difference between a series circuit and a parallel circuit?

3 What Is a Magnet?

A magnet is an object that attracts certain metals. A magnet has a magnetic field. A magnet has magnetic poles.

Properties of Magnets

A **magnet** (MAG niht) is an object that attracts some metals. A magnet mainly attracts iron. This property of magnets to attract metal is called magnetism. Magnetism is stronger the closer a magnet is to an object with iron in it. The closer the magnet gets, the stronger the pull becomes.

Magnets do not attract all metals. Magnets do not attract materials such as wood or rubber. Some magnets keep their magnetism a long time. You can use these magnets to magnetize other objects. But these kinds of magnetized objects lose their magnetism after a while.

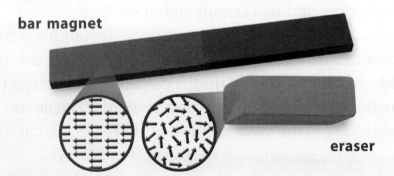

bar magnet

eraser

Particles of matter act like tiny magnets. When particles of an object line up, the object is a magnet.

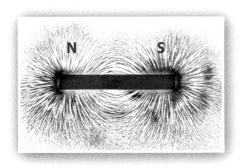

UNLIKE POLES ATTRACT
The north pole of one magnet pulls toward the south pole of another magnet.

MAGNETIC FIELD
Small pieces of iron show the lines of force around a magnet.

LIKE POLES REPEL
The south pole of one magnet pushes away from the south pole of another magnet.

Magnetic Fields

Magnetism is a force. The space in which a magnet's force can act is called its magnetic field (MAG nehtik feeld). Each magnet has two **magnetic poles** where the magnet's force is greatest. Look at the picture of a magnetic field. The pieces of iron are thicker and closer together at each end of the bar magnet.

When a bar magnet can swing freely, one end always points north. This end of the magnet is its north pole. The other end points south. This is its south pole.

Remember what you learned about electric charges. Opposite charges attract each other. Magnets act the same way. The unlike poles of two magnets attract each other. The like poles of two magnets repel each other.

Earth as a Magnet

The center of the Earth is made up mostly of melted iron. As Earth spins, the iron particles line up. Imagine Earth with a giant bar magnet inside. This means Earth has a magnetic force field around it.

The needle of a magnetic compass is a permanent magnet. The needle can turn freely. One end of a compass needle always turns to find north. That is how people can use compasses to know which direction is north. Sailors use magnetic compasses to find their way across oceans.

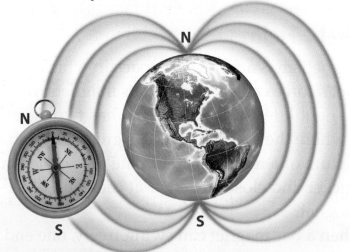

EARTH'S MAGNETIC FIELD
Earth acts like a giant magnet. A compass always points toward Earth's magnetic north pole.

MAIN IDEA AND DETAILS

What will happen if you bring the unlike poles of two magnets near each other?

4 How Do Electromagnets Work?

Magnetism can produce electricity. Electricity can produce magnetism. Together, magnetism and electricity can produce energy of motion.

Electromagnets

An **electromagnet** (ih lehk troh MAG niht) is a strong temporary magnet. It uses electricity to produce magnetism. How does electricity produce magnetism?

You know electric current flows through a conductor, such as a wire. As it flows, it creates a magnetic field around the wire. This magnetic field is weak. If the wire is wrapped around a piece of iron, the iron becomes magnetized. The magnetic field becomes stronger.

Many things in your home have electromagnets in them. Small electromagnets are inside such things as blenders, computer disk drives, and doorbells.

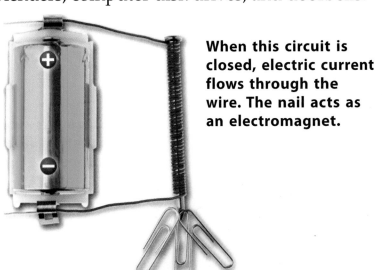

When this circuit is closed, electric current flows through the wire. The nail acts as an electromagnet.

Using Electromagnets

Like other magnets, electromagnets attract materials made of iron. They also have magnetic fields. Electromagnets can be very small. Some can fit in your hand. Even small electromagnets can be very strong.

The magnetic force of an electromagnet can be controlled. You can make its magnetic field stronger. If more wire is wrapped around iron, the electromagnet becomes stronger. If more electric current flows through the wire, the electromagnet becomes stronger.

An electromagnet can be turned on and off. It only acts like a magnet when electric current flows through the wire. When the electric current is turned off, the electromagnet loses its magnetism. Electromagnets are very useful. A crane uses an electromagnet to pick up cars and other heavy objects that contain iron.

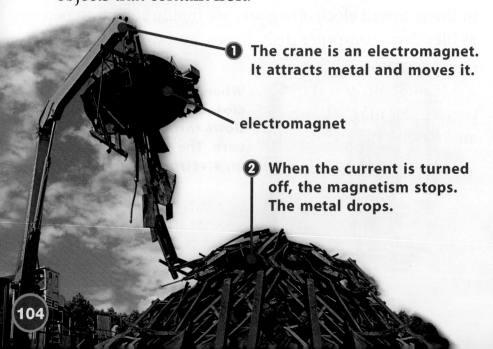

❶ The crane is an electromagnet. It attracts metal and moves it.

electromagnet

❷ When the current is turned off, the magnetism stops. The metal drops.

Motors

An electric **motor** is a machine that changes electrical energy into energy of motion. All electric motors have electromagnets and permanent magnets.

In an electric motor, wires are wrapped around an iron core called a shaft. Electric current runs through the wires. The shaft becomes an electromagnet. Around the electromagnet is a permanent magnet.

Remember what you know about magnetic fields. Like poles repel. Unlike poles attract. The magnetic fields of the electromagnet and the permanent magnet attract and repel. This creates the energy of motion.

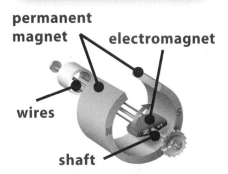

permanent magnet   electromagnet

wires

shaft

❶ In a motor, electricity flows through an electromagnet. The current keeps changing direction.

❷ The permanent magnet repels and attracts the electromagnet. This turns the shaft of the motor.

❸ As the shaft of the motor turns, electrical energy changes to energy of motion.

Generating Electricity

You have learned that an electric motor uses magnetism to change electrical energy into energy of motion. A generator does the opposite of an electric motor. A **generator** (JEHN uh ray tuhr) uses magnetism to change energy of motion into electrical energy.

From Generator to Customer

ENERGY SOURCE
Energy from falling water or burning fuel helps generators produce electricity.

ELECTRIC POWER LINES
Power lines carry electricity to customers.

Giant generators produce the electricity that lights up whole cities and runs machines. These generators have permanent magnets with lots of power. They have huge loops of wire. The loops move across the magnetic field of the permanent magnet. This produces electric current in the wires.

Energy in motion moves the wire loops of a generator. This energy can come from such things as burning coal, steam, falling water, or wind.

HOMES AND BUSINESSES
Electricity is used every day.

The Cost of Using Electricity

Using electricity costs money. You pay for how much electricity you use. Each month, you get an electric bill for the total amount of electricity you have used in your home.

The cost of using an electric machine depends on two things. One is the amount of time it is used. The other is the amount of electrical energy it needs to run.

Some machines use electricity only part of the time. Examples are fans and washing machines. Other machines use electricity 24 hours a day, every day. Examples are refrigerators and clocks. The graph shows the average monthly cost of using some everyday machines.

A fan only uses electricity when it is turned on.

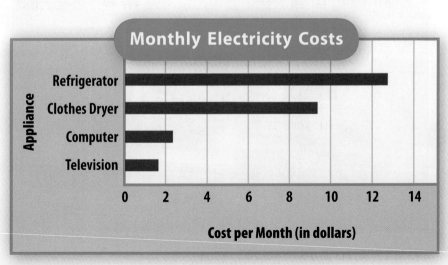

Monthly Electricity Costs

Which of these uses the most electricity each month?

A computer still uses electricity when it is resting or turned off.

Some electric machines use electricity even when you are not using them! If a computer were left on "sleep" for an entire year, it would still use about $40 worth of electricity.

Some things have built-in clocks. The clocks run on electricity even if the machine is turned off. Look at your radio, DVD player, or stereo. Do they have a clock that is on all the time, even if you are not using the machine? This use of electricity costs money.

Follow these tips to save electricity:

• Use a safety cord to plug in TVs, DVD players, and other machines. When the switch is turned off, no electricity reaches the machines.

• Turn your computer off instead of letting it sleep.

• Turn off lights, TVs, and stereos when you are not in the room.

COMPARE AND CONTRAST

How do a refrigerator and a washing machine differ in their use of electricity?

Glossary

conductors (kuhn DUHK tuhrz) Materials that negatively charged particles can move through easily.

electric cell (ih LEHK trihk sehl) A device that turns chemical energy into electrical energy.

electric charges (ih LEHK trihk CHAHRJ ehs) Tiny particles that carry units of electricity.

electric circuit (ih LEHK trihk SUR kiht) The pathway that an electric current follows.

electric current (ih LEHK trihk KUR uhnt) A continuous flow of electric charges.

electromagnet (ih lehk troh MAG niht) A strong temporary magnet that uses electricity to produce magnetism.

generator (JEHN uh ray tuhr) A devise that uses magnetism to convert energy of motion into electrical energy.

Glossary

insulators (IHN suh lay tuhrz) Materials that electric charges do not flow through easily.

magnet (MAG niht) An object that attracts certain metals, mainly iron.

magnetic poles (mag NEHT ihk pohlz) The two areas on a magnet with the greatest magnetic force.

motor (MOH tur) A device that changes electrical energy into energy of motion.

parallel circuit (PAR uh lehl SUR kiht) A circuit in which the parts are connected so that the electric current passes along more than one pathway.

series circuit (SIHR eez SUR kiht) A circuit in which the parts are connected so that the electric current passes through each part along a single pathway.

static electricity (STAT ihk ih lehk TRIHS ih tee) An electric charge that builds up on a material.

Think About What You Have Read

Vocabulary

❶ A constant flow of electric charges is called _____ .

   A) magnetism

   B) electric current

   C) power lines

   D) a conductor

Comprehension

❷ When does an object have an overall positive charge?

❸ Explain why a switch might be added to a circuit. Give examples.

❹ Why don't magnets attract wooden objects?

Critical Thinking

❺ You reach for a doorknob and get a small shock. Use what you know about static electricity to explain why this happened.

Motion and Machines

Contents

1 How Can Motion Be Described?

You can describe the motion of an object. You can tell its speed and its direction. Speed and direction together set an object's velocity.

Position and Motion

Position (puh ZIHSH uhn) is an object's location, or place. For example, the position of your desk in the classroom might be 2 m (6.6 ft) from the wall. Motion (MOH shuhn) is a change in an object's position as compared to objects around it. If you move your desk, its position changes. Its position changes as compared to the wall of the classroom.

An object can appear to be moving when compared to some objects. An object can also appear not to be moving when compared to other objects.

The car is moving. As its position changes, it moves farther away from the sign.

Look at the photo of the children in the car. Compared to each other, the children are not moving. Compared to the car they are in, the children are not moving. But when compared to objects outside the car, the children are moving. Their positions are changing compared with the sign and the trees. The objects used to compare motion are called a frame of reference.

When you are standing still, Earth is still moving. From your frame of reference, you do not think Earth is moving because you move right along with it. An astronaut in space has a different frame of reference. From space, Earth seems to move. Its position changes when compared to other objects in space.

The children in the car can tell they are moving by looking out the window to see that they are passing signs and trees.

Measuring Motion

How long would it take you to walk 10 km? How long would it take you to go 10 km in a car? A car can move at a higher speed. This means you can travel the same distance in a shorter amount of time in a car.

Speed is a measure of the distance an object travels in a certain amount of time. Speed is measured using units of distance and time. For example, you might measure speed by kilometers traveled in an hour.

You can find the speed of an object if you know two things. You need to know the distance the object traveled. You also need to know how long it took the object to go that distance.

Each runner runs the same distance. The fastest runner has the shortest time.

A runner's speed is measured using units of distance and time.

2-km Race Results

Runner 1	8 min 32 s
Runner 2	10 min 50 s
Runner 3	11 min 59 s

You divide distance by time to find speed. Think of a car traveling 100 km in 2 hours. You find its speed by dividing distance by time. Its speed is 100 km divided by 2 hours. Its speed is 50 km an hour.

The runners shown travel the same distance. However, they finish the race at different times. A runner who finishes the race in a shorter amount of time has a faster speed.

Every motion has a speed. Some objects move very slowly. Most glaciers move downhill just a few meters in a year. Other objects move very quickly. The wings of a hummingbird move so quickly they are just a blur.

Describing Direction

Each motion has a direction as well as a speed. Direction tells you which way an object is moving. You can talk about direction in many ways. You can use words such as *east, west, north, south, right, left, up,* or *down.*

Velocity (vuh LAHS ih tee) is a measure of speed in a certain direction. Speed and direction together determine, or set, velocity. The bicyclists shown change direction the whole time they go around the curve. Their speed may not change. Even so, their change of direction causes their velocity to change.

Forces such as friction and gravity can also change the velocity of moving objects.

The people on bicycles go around a curve. They change direction as they go around the curve. This changes their velocity.

TEXT STRUCTURE

Why does the word *velocity* appear in boldface, or dark type?

2 What Are Gravity and Friction?

Forces are pushes or pulls that cause objects to change their motion. Friction and gravity are two important natural forces.

Pushes and Pulls

You push a heavy box across a floor. You pull a wagon behind you. You use pushes and pulls to make objects change their motion.

A **force** (fawrs) is a push or a pull. A push is a force that moves an object away. A pull is a force that moves an object nearer. Look at the girl in the picture. She is using a force to pull.

PULL As the girl pulls on the rake, the leaves move toward her.

pull

push

PUSH As the boy pushes the wheelbarrow, it moves away from him.

A force can change the motion of an object. A force can start an object moving. A force can change the direction or speed of an object. A force can stop an object from moving.

Think about moving a heavy box across the floor. The box has no motion until you push it. It moves in one direction as you push it in that direction. You can change the speed of the box. You do that by using a different force. You must push the box harder to move it faster. You would also have to push harder on a box with a greater mass in order to move it.

You can change the direction of the box by using a different force. You must push the box from a different side. Or you must push the box from a different direction. You can stop the box from moving if you stop pushing it.

Friction

When you stop pushing a heavy box, a different force stops the box from sliding. That force is called friction (FRIHK shuhn). **Friction** is a force that slows or stops motion between two surfaces that touch each other.

There is more friction between rough surfaces. There is less friction between smooth surfaces. So there is some friction between a box and a smooth tile floor. There is more friction between a box and a rough concrete floor.

Friction between the brake and the wheel stops the wheel from turning when the brake is used.

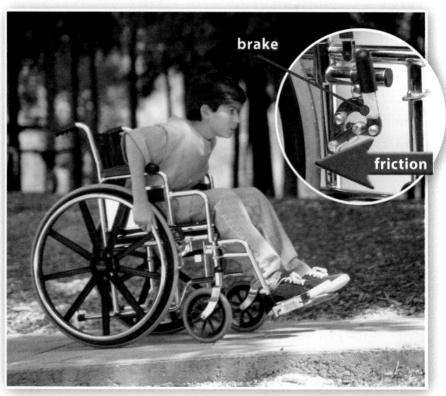

brake

friction

Friction can be useful. Without friction, you would slip and slide. Friction helps you hold a pencil. Without friction, you would not be able to write. The pencil would slip out of your hand.

There is even friction between objects and the air. This is called air resistance. You can feel air resistance when you ride a bicycle.

Friction slows or stops movement. This can sometimes be useful. A wheelchair stays in place because of the friction between the wheel and the brake. But sometimes less friction is better. For example, less friction between snow and a snowboard lets the snowboard go faster.

There is very little friction between snow and a snowboard. You can slide down a hill on a snowboard.

Friction between wheels and the sidewalk helps skaters control their speed and direction.

There are ways to create less friction between objects. One way is to put slippery matter on surfaces that touch. You can put slippery wax on the bottom of the snowboard. This makes less friction between a snowboard and the snow. This makes the snowboard go faster.

Wheels also reduce, or make less, friction. Wheels roll over a surface instead of sliding on it. Some machines use small rolling metal balls between their surfaces. This reduces friction between moving parts. These balls are called ball bearings.

This race car was built to have less friction with the air. Its smooth shape helps it move faster.

Some moving objects are built to have less friction with the air. This helps them move faster through the air. Race cars and airplanes have smooth shapes. This helps the air slide over them. Runners wear smooth, tight-fitting clothing for the same reason.

Friction is one natural force that makes objects change their motion. Friction acts on objects that are touching each other.

Gravity

Gravity (GRAV ih tee) is a force that pulls objects toward each other. Earth's gravity pulls skydivers toward the ground. Gravity also keeps your books on your desk. It makes rain fall from the clouds.

Gravity can act on objects that are close or at a distance. Earth's gravity can even act on objects in space. Gravity holds the Moon in orbit around Earth. Objects with greater mass have greater gravity. Earth has more mass than the Moon. Earth's gravity is stronger than the Moon's gravity.

When people landed on the Moon, they could jump higher and lift heavier objects than they could on Earth. That is because the Moon's gravity is weaker.

Gravity pulls these skydivers toward Earth.

CAUSE AND EFFECT

What is one way to reduce friction?

3 How Do Simple Machines Work?

Simple machines help people do work by changing a force.

Six Simple Machines

When you open a can using a pull tab, you are using a machine. A machine is any tool that makes work easier. A **simple machine** (SIHM puhl muh SHEEN) is an object that changes a force. A simple machine lets you use less force to move an object.

Some simple machines change the direction of the force. Some simple machines increase the distance over which a force is used.

A paddle is a simple machine.

paddle

Inclined Plane

An **inclined plane** (ihn KLYND playn) is a simple machine. It is made up of a slanted surface. A ramp is an inclined plane. An inclined plane increases the distance over which a force is used. It makes work easier.

You might want to move a heavy box up to the top of a ramp. It is hard to lift a heavy box straight up to the top. It is easier to push the heavy box up a long ramp to the top.

more force

less force

This ramp is an inclined plane. Using the ramp makes it easier to move the box to the top of the ramp.

A knife is a wedge.

downward force

outward force

Wedge

A **wedge** (wehj) is a simple machine made up of two inclined planes. A wedge is shaped like a V. A wedge changes the direction of a force. It changes a downward force to an outward force. This helps to cut objects or to split objects apart.

Screw

A **screw** (skroo) is a simple machine made up of an inclined plane wrapped around a post. A screw changes the direction of a force. It changes a turning force to a downward force. The turning force is weak. The downward force is strong.

Turning a screw with a screwdriver pushes the screw into wood. It is easy to turn the screw. The force is spread out over many turns.

The threads of a screw are an inclined plane. The turning force of a screw easily pushes it into wood.

less force

more force

more
force

less
force

**This screwdriver is being used as a lever.
A lever makes it easier to lift the lid.**

Lever

A **lever** (LEHV ur) is a simple machine made up
of a stiff bar that moves freely on a fixed point. The
fixed point a lever moves on is called the fulcrum
(FUL kruhm). The fulcrum is usually placed close to
one end of the lever. This makes one end of the lever
longer than the other end.

Examples of levers include seesaws and can
openers. Levers are often used to help lift objects.
A small force is used on the long end of a lever.
This creates a large force at the short end of the lever.
This makes the work of lifting things much easier.

Wheel and Axle

A **wheel and axle** (hweel and AK suhl) is a simple machine made up of two cylinders that turn on the same axis. Using a wheel and axle makes work easier. A larger wheel turns on the smaller wheel, or axle.

Examples of wheels and axles include car steering wheels and doorknobs. A small force is used to turn the large wheel. This creates a large force that moves the axle. By using a wheel and axle, less force is needed to steer a car or to open a door.

A faucet is a wheel and axle. You use a small force to turn the wheel. This creates a large force that turns the axle.

less force

more force

Pulley

A simple machine made up of a rope fitted around the rim of a fixed wheel is called a **pulley** (PUL ee). Some pulleys increase the force that is used on them. Others change the direction of the force.

Changing the direction of a force to the opposite direction can be useful. A flagpole pulley changes a downward force to an upward force. To use a pulley, you pull down on one end of the pulley rope. The rope turns the wheel at the top of the flagpole. The turning wheel makes the rope change direction. The rope can then pull up the flag.

Pulleys are also used to raise and lower elevator cars.

You pull down on one end of the rope of a pulley. The other end of the rope pulls the flag up the pole.

A simple machine helps you do work. But a pulley or any other machine can break. Then it may not work correctly. If the parts of a machine do not match, the machine may not work correctly.

For example, the rope of a pulley might be wider than the rim of the pulley wheel. Then the rope might slip off the pulley when you pull on it. The pulley would not be able to do its job.

A knife can get dull. A dull knife does not work correctly. It does not help you do work.

PROBLEM-SOLUTION

What simple machine could be used to split a log into smaller pieces?

Glossary

force (fawrs) A push that moves an object away or a pull that moves an object nearer.

friction (FRIHK shuhn) A force that slows or stops motion between two surfaces that are touching.

gravity (GRAV ih tee) The force that pulls bodies or objects toward other bodies or objects.

inclined plane (ihn KLYND playn) A simple machine made up of a slanted surface.

lever (LEHV ur) A simple machine made up of a stiff bar that moves freely around a fixed point.

motion (MOH shuhn) A change in an object's position as compared to objects around it.

position (puh ZIHSH uhn) An object's location, or place.

Glossary

pulley (PUL ee) A simple machine made up of a rope fitted around the rim of a fixed wheel.

screw (skroo) A simple machine made up of an inclined plane wrapped around a column.

simple machine (SIHM puhl muh SHEEN) A device that changes a force.

speed (speed) A measure of the distance an object travels in a certain amount of time.

velocity (vuh LAHS ih tee) A measure of speed in a certain direction.

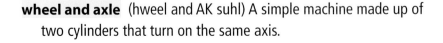

wedge (wehj) A simple machine made up of two inclined planes.

wheel and axle (hweel and AK suhl) A simple machine made up of two cylinders that turn on the same axis.

Think About What You Have Read

Vocabulary

❶ Which statement is true about gravity?

A) It acts only on objects that are touching.

B) It can act over a distance.

C) It is a pushing force.

D) Only very large objects have it.

Comprehension

❷ What two properties describe the motion of an object?

❸ Give two examples of forces.

❹ How do simple machines help people do work?

Critical Thinking

❺ Choose a sport or other activity you enjoy. Describe the different forces—pushes, pulls, gravity, and friction—that you use during the activity.

Forces That Shape Earth's Surface

Contents

1 What Is the Rock Cycle?

The top layer of Earth is made up of rock. Over time, one kind of rock can be changed into another kind of rock.

Earth's Layers

Earth is made up of layers. If you could take a part out of Earth, you would see the layers. The outer layer is the **crust**. The ocean floor and all the land on Earth are part of the crust.

The crust is the thinnest layer of Earth. It is made up of rock. **Rock** is a solid material made up of one or more minerals (MIHN ur uhlz). A **mineral** is a solid material found in Earth's crust that has a definite chemical makeup.

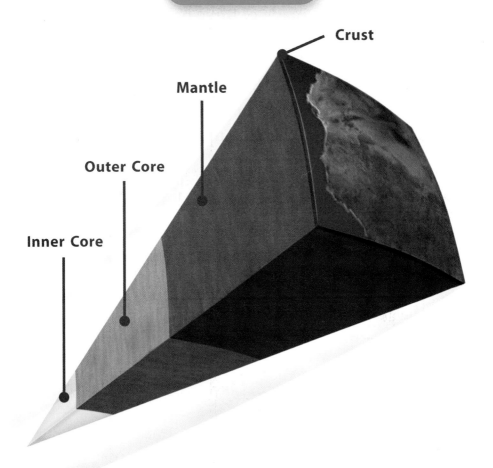

Crust

Mantle

Outer Core

Inner Core

The next layer of Earth is the mantle (MAN tl). The **mantle** is a thick layer of rock beneath the crust. In the upper part of the mantle, the rock is melted and soft. This is called molten rock. The lower part of the mantle is solid.

In the center of Earth is the core (kawr). The **core** is a ball with two parts. The outer part is liquid, and the inner part is solid. The solid inner part is the hottest part of Earth.

Rocks of Earth's Crust

Earth's crust is made of three basic kinds of rock. Each kind forms in a different way. Each kind has different features.

The first kind of rock is igneous (IHG nee uhs) rock. You know that there is molten, or melted, rock in Earth's mantle. When the molten rock cools and hardens, it forms **igneous rock**.

Sometimes molten rock cools slowly inside Earth's crust. Sometimes molten rock flows from an opening in the crust. A volcano (vahl KAY noh) is such an opening. This molten rock cools quickly.

molten rock

volcano

There are different types of igneous rock. The molten rock contains different minerals. As the rock cools and hardens, these minerals form crystals (KRIHS tuhlz). For example, diamond is a crystal.

Igneous Rock

Obsidian (ahb SIHD ee uhn) forms when molten rock cools quickly.

Basalt (buh SAWLT) makes up much of Earth's crust beneath the oceans.

Granite (GRAN iht) forms when molten rock gets hard in the crust.

Molten rock gets hard to form igneous rock.

Sedimentary Rock

Conglomerate (kuhn GLAHM ur iht) forms from sediments of different sizes.

Some limestone forms when the remains of ocean animals pack together.

Shale forms from thin layers of clay.

Bits of sand, rock, and once-living things settle and pack together to make sedimentary rock.

The second kind of rock is sedimentary (sehd uh MEHN tuh ree) rock. Bits of sand, rock, soil, and the remains of once-living things mix together and make **sediment** (SEHD uh muhnt). **Sedimentary rock** forms when sediment hardens.

Wind, moving water, and moving ice carry sediment. Then it settles in low places. It slowly packs together. Dissolved minerals fill in any cracks and glue the pieces together. Sedimentary rock is formed.

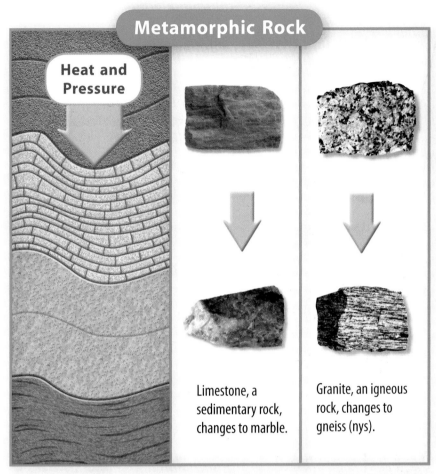

Heat, pressure, or chemicals change some rocks into metamorphic rocks.

The third kind of rock is metamorphic (meht uh MAWR fihk) rock. Metamorphic rock forms beneath Earth's surface. **Metamorphic rock** is new rock that forms when existing rocks are changed by heat, pressure, or chemicals.

Igneous and sedimentary rocks can be changed into metamorphic rock. Metamorphic rocks can also be changed to make new metamorphic rock.

The Rock Cycle

sediments

CEMENTING Dissolved minerals fill in cracks between sediments.

Weathering

sedimentary rock

WEATHERING Wind, moving water, and ice break rocks into sediment.

Weathering

HEAT AND PRESSURE Metamorphic rocks form through heat and pressure.

igneous rock

Heat and Pressure

metamorphic rock

COOLING AND HARDENING Molten rock cools and gets hard to form igneous rock.

molten rock

MELTING Rocks melt from great heat.

How Rocks Change

Remember that there are three basic kinds of rock. The three basic kinds are igneous rock, sedimentary rock, and metamorphic rock. Any kind of rock can change into another kind. For example, metamorphic rock can become sedimentary rock.

Rocks may seem too hard to break or change, but they do. Wind, moving water, and ice can break rocks into pieces. This is called weathering.

Scientists call the changes rocks go through the **rock cycle**. The rock cycle never ends. Rocks build up and wear away again and again.

CLASSIFY

Classify limestone, marble, and obsidian by how they are made.

2 What Are Rapid Surface Changes?

Earth's surface is always changing. Earthquakes, volcanoes, and landslides cause rapid, or fast, changes to Earth's surface.

Earthquakes

Earth's crust seems solid, but it is cracked in some places. A crack in Earth's crust is called a fault (fawlt). Earthquakes take place along a fault. An earthquake (URTH kwayk) is a sudden movement of part of Earth's crust.

Parts of Earth's crust are moving very slowly. Sometimes the parts of the crust come together, move apart, or slide past each other. When the parts hit each other, it often causes an earthquake.

The San Andreas fault is a crack in Earth's crust. Earthquakes often occur there.

fault

A strong earthquake in Kobe, Japan caused parts of the highway to fall.

Earth's crust is always changing. Forces deep inside Earth push on the rock above. This pushing may build up for many years. Sometimes the pushing on the rock becomes too great. Then the parts on either side of a fault may move suddenly. This sudden movement is an earthquake.

The strength of an earthquake relates to the amount of pushing. When the pushing is very great, a strong earthquake takes place.

During an earthquake, the movement of the rock can create landforms. Mountains are pushed up. Valleys can form. New faults can form, too.

Volcanoes

A volcano is an opening in Earth's crust. When a volcano erupts, hot ash, gases, and molten rock escape from deep inside Earth. The molten rock beneath Earth's surface is called **magma** (MAG muh). The molten rock that reaches Earth's surface is called **lava** (LAH vuh).

It is very hot deep within Earth's mantle. It is so hot in some places that rocks melt. The melted rocks are magma. As magma rises, some of it gets hard and becomes igneous rock. Some magma pushes its way through a fault to Earth's surface. It flows onto Earth's surface as lava.

Volcanoes can erupt in different ways. Thick, slow-moving lava erupts from some volcanoes. Other volcanoes erupt suddenly. They can quickly change Earth's surface.

A Volcano Erupts

Hot lava, gases, and rock flow from the volcano.

Lava cools and gets hard.

Magma pushes toward Earth's surface.

Pressure pushes magma upward.

Mount St. Helens is a volcano in the state of Washington. On May 18, 1980, Mount St. Helens erupted. Ash and hot gases blew through the air. The heat melted the snow on the mountainside. Rocks, soil, mud, and water crashed down. Forests for many miles were completely destroyed!

Mount St. Helens looked like this before it erupted in 1980.

Mount St. Helens began to erupt in March 1980.

The major eruption in May 1980 lasted for nine hours.

After the eruption, the land was completely changed.

Landslides

When Mount St. Helens erupted, it caused a huge mudslide. A landslide is the sudden movement of loose rock and soil down a steep slope. If the soil is soaked with water, the landslide is called a mudslide.

Earthquakes and volcanic eruptions can cause landslides and mudslides. Heavy rains or the sudden melting of snow can cause mudslides. A mudslide can carry away trees, boulders, cars, and even houses.

CAUSE AND EFFECT

Identify three effects that an earthquake may have on the land.

3

What Are Slow Surface Changes?

Earth's surface is slowly built up and worn down. Weathering, erosion, deposition, and mountain building make slow changes to Earth's surface.

Weathering

Moving water can make rocks tumble and bump against each other. The rocks bump over and over again. The rocks wear down. Sharp edges become smooth and the rocks get smaller. This is an example of weathering (WETH ur ihng).

Weathering is the slow wearing away of rock into smaller pieces. Moving water, ice, plant roots, and chemicals are causes of weathering.

Ocean waves wear away rock to form sea stacks.

The roots of plants can break rocks.

Most rocks have tiny cracks in them. In places where it gets cold, water can get in the cracks and freeze. Ice makes the cracks bigger. Periods of freezing and melting can cause rocks to break.

The same kind of thing happens when plant roots grow into cracks in a rock. The growing roots push open the cracks. After some time the rock breaks.

Chemicals can also weather rocks. Some gases in the air combine with rain to make acid rain. Acid rain can cause rocks to break.

Erosion

You know that weathering is the slow wearing away of rock into smaller pieces. Erosion (ih ROH zhuhn) carries away the small pieces of rock. **Erosion** is the movement of rock material from one place to another.

Water is the main cause of erosion. When water flows over soil, it picks up tiny pieces of the soil. When the water moves downhill, it carries the tiny pieces with it.

Erosion of rock takes a very long time. First, the water of a fast-moving river cuts a dip into the rock. Then the running water carries away more and more material. Over a great many years, a deep canyon forms. That is how the Grand Canyon in Arizona was formed.

This balanced rock formed after many years of weathering and erosion.

Wind is another cause of erosion. In some places, there are few plants. Plants are needed to hold soil in place. Without plants, the wind easily picks up dry soil. If you have ever been to the beach on a windy day, you have felt the wind blowing the sand. Wind carries away dry sand and soil.

Erosion is also caused by glaciers (GLAY shurz). A glacier is a large sheet of slow-moving ice. As it moves, a glacier can dig out huge areas of rock and soil. A glacier can dig out a valley or a canyon.

A moving glacier dug out the long valley.

Deposition

Erosion moves bits of sand, soil, and rock. Where do these bits go? Remember that these bits are called sediment. The dropping of sediment after it is moved is called **deposition** (dehp uh ZIHSH uhn). There are three main causes of deposition—wind, glaciers, and moving water.

The wind picks up and carries dry sand. When the wind stops, the sand drops. Sand dunes are made by wind and deposition.

As glaciers move, they carry rocks and soil. A melting glacier drops the rocks and soil.

Oceans and rivers also cause deposition. Ocean waves wear away some beaches. New beaches are made through deposition.

Rivers slow down as they flow into a lake or ocean. Sediment settles when the moving water slows. The sediment can build up at the mouth of the river. This makes a landform called a delta.

Delta

Sand dunes

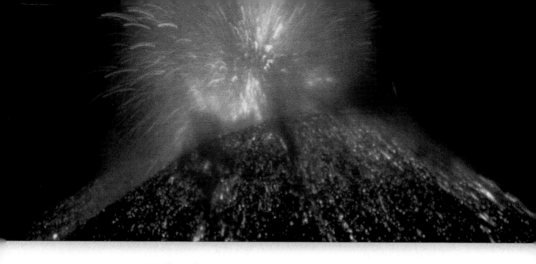

Mountain Building

Mountains form in different ways. A volcano can make a mountain very quickly. Other mountains form as parts of Earth's crust move. This happens slowly, over millions of years.

Sometimes huge parts of Earth's crust crash together. The crust gets pushed up and folded. The Himalayas (hihm uh LAY uhz) are folded mountains.

Some mountains form along a fault. Parts of Earth's crust move upward along the fault. The Sierra Nevadas in California and Nevada are fault-block mountains.

Mountains may form without folding or faulting. Pressure simply pushes up Earth's crust. The Adirondack Mountains in New York were made this way.

MAIN IDEA

How does erosion form a deep canyon?

Glossary

core (kawr) The innermost layer of Earth.

crust (kruhst) The outermost layer of Earth.

deposition (dehp uh ZIHSH uhn) The dropping of sediment moved by water, wind, and ice.

erosion (ih ROH zhuhn) The movement of rock material from one place to another.

igneous rock (IHG nee uhs rahk) The type of rock that is formed when melted rock from inside Earth cools and hardens.

lava (LAH vuh) Molten rock that reaches Earth's surface, such as when a volcano erupts.

magma (MAG muh) Molten rock beneath Earth's surface.

mantle (MAN tl) A thick layer of rock between Earth's crust and core.

Glossary

metamorphic rock (meht uh MAWR fihk rahk)
New rock that forms when existing rocks are
changed by heat, pressure, or chemicals.

mineral (MIHN ur uhl) A solid, nonliving material of specific
chemical makeup.

rock (rahk) A solid material that is made up of one or more minerals.

rock cycle (rahk SY kuhl) The continuous series of changes that rocks
go through.

sediment (SEHD uh muhnt) Sand, particles of rock, bits of soil, and
the remains of once-living things.

sedimentary rock (sehd uh MEHN tuh ree
rahk) A type of rock that forms when
sediment becomes pressed together
and hardens.

weathering (WEHTH ur ihng) The slow wearing
away of rock into smaller pieces.

Think About What You Have Read

Vocabulary

❶ The thick layer of rock between the crust and the core is called the _____ .

A) lava

B) core

C) magma

D) mantle

Comprehension

❷ Layers of mud and clay settle and get hard to form rock. How would you classify this rock?

❸ What are three ways that Earth's surface can change quickly?

❹ What are three ways that slowly change Earth's surface?

Critical Thinking

❺ Suppose you interview someone who witnessed a volcanic eruption. What questions would you ask in order to learn as much as possible about the eruption?

Using Weather Data

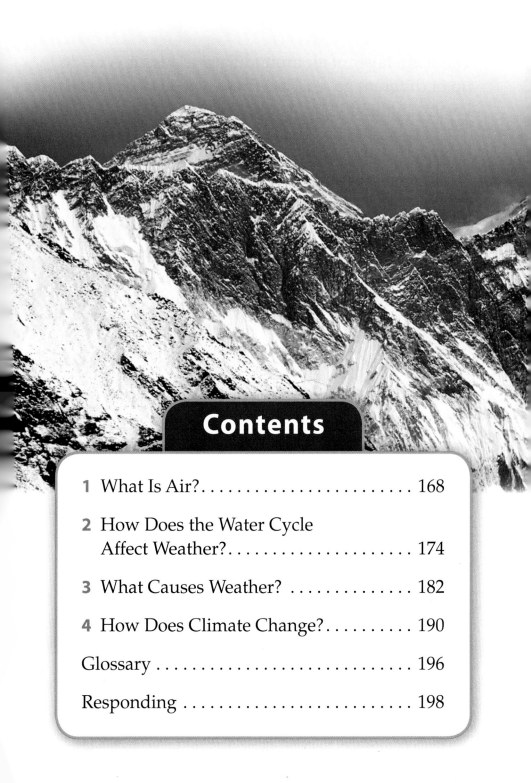

Contents

1 What Is Air?

There is a layer of air around Earth. This air is made up of different gases. These gases are important to Earth's living things.

Gases in Air

Did you ever wonder what is in the air you breathe? Air is made up of gases that have no color or smell. Air is all around Earth. The largest part of air is a gas called nitrogen (NY truh juhn). The next largest part of air is a gas called oxygen (AHK sih juhn). Living things need oxygen to live. Your body needs oxygen to use the fuel in the food you eat. Most living things get the oxygen they need from air.

Nitrogen and oxygen are not the only gases that make up air. Small amounts of other things are found in air, too. Two of these things are carbon dioxide (KAHR-buhn dy-AHK syd) and water.

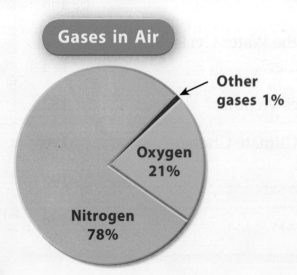

Gases in Air

Other gases 1%

Oxygen 21%

Nitrogen 78%

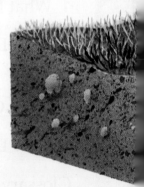

Carbon dioxide is a gas that helps hold heat close to Earth. It has no color or odor. People give off carbon dioxide when they breathe. Animals give off carbon dioxide when they breathe. Plants use carbon dioxide to make food. When plants make food, they give off oxygen.

Animals use oxygen to get energy from food. Animals give off carbon dioxide.

Plants use carbon dioxide in air to make food. When plants make food, they put oxygen into the air.

Plants need nitrogen to grow. Plants take in nitrogen through their roots.

Earth's Blanket

On a cold night, it is good to have a blanket. Earth has a blanket, too. It is a layer of gases called the **atmosphere** (AT muh sfihr). The Sun heats Earth. The atmosphere holds the heat close to Earth's surface.

Like all matter, air takes up space. Air also has weight. The weight of air presses down on Earth all the time. This weight is called **air pressure** (PREHSH uhr).

High in the mountains there is less air pressing down on Earth. This means air pressure on a mountaintop is lower than it is at the bottom of the mountain.

Air is thin high in the mountains. Climbers carry oxygen with them to breathe.

The atmosphere has four layers. The lowest layer is called the troposphere (TROHP uh sfihr). This layer begins at Earth's surface. Earth's weather occurs in this first layer. **Weather** is the conditions of the atmosphere at a certain place and time.

The next layer of the atmosphere is the stratosphere (STRAT uh sfihr). Airplanes travel in this layer. This layer keeps a lot of the harmful part of the Sun's rays from reaching Earth.

The mesosphere (MEHZ uh sfihr) is the next layer of the atmosphere. The coldest temperatures in the atmosphere are found here.

The top layer of the atmosphere is called the thermosphere (THUHRM uh sfihr). Space shuttles travel in this layer.

Thermosphere

Mesosphere

Stratosphere

Troposphere

Greenhouse Effect

If you have ever been in a greenhouse, you know it is warm inside. The air in a greenhouse is usually warmer than the air outside. The glass walls and roof of a greenhouse let in light and heat from the Sun. The glass traps the heat. It lets little heat out. This keeps the plants inside warm.

The atmosphere keeps Earth warm in the same way. Earth's atmosphere lets in light and heat from the Sun. Some of the heat escapes into space. But the atmosphere holds most of the heat in.

This natural heating of Earth is called the greenhouse effect. The **greenhouse effect** is the process by which heat from the Sun builds up near Earth's surface. The atmosphere then traps the heat there. In recent years, carbon dioxide and other harmful gases have begun to build up in the atmosphere. Some scientists warn that this build up of gases will cause Earth's air to become warmer. This is called global warming.

A greenhouse keeps plants warm on cold days.

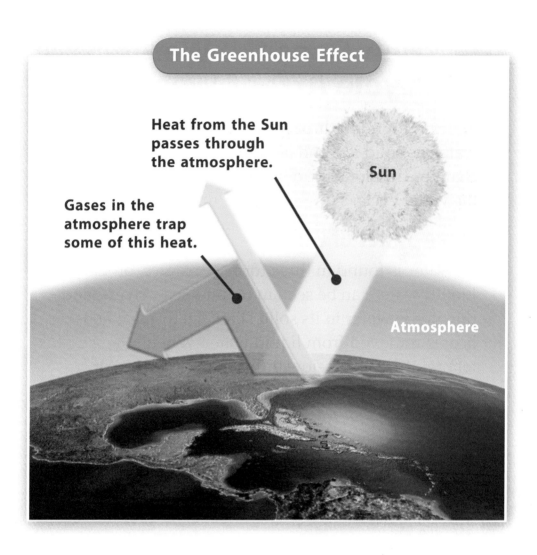

The Greenhouse Effect

Heat from the Sun passes through the atmosphere.

Sun

Gases in the atmosphere trap some of this heat.

Atmosphere

TEXT STRUCTURE

Use the diagram to explain the greenhouse effect.

2 How Does the Water Cycle Affect Weather?

Water is found in three forms on Earth—as liquid water, as solid ice, and as water vapor. Water changes from one form to another in a process called the water cycle.

Three States of Water

Water is found in three forms, or states, on Earth. Liquid water can be seen in oceans, seas, rivers, and rain. Ice is water in its solid state. Ice forms when heat is removed from liquid water. When temperatures fall below 0°C (32°F), liquid water becomes ice.

Water in gas form is called water vapor (VAY pur). Water vapor is in the air, but you cannot see it. It forms when heat is added to liquid water.

Some parts of this lake are frozen.

ice

When heat is added to ice, it melts. It changes to liquid water. Heat from the Sun melts ice on the lake shown below. Heat can also change liquid water to water vapor. This change is called evaporation (ih VAP uh ray shuhn). **Evaporation** happens when a liquid changes to a gas.

The mist you see above the lake is not water vapor. It is a cloud of tiny drops of water. The drops formed by condensation (kahn-dehn SAY shun). **Condensation** happens when gas changes to liquid. The water vapor came from lake water that evaporated. When the air above the lake cooled, the water vapor condensed. It became a liquid again.

water vapor

liquid water

The Water Cycle

The water on Earth changes from one form to another over and over again. This is called the water cycle (SY kuhl). The **water cycle** is the movement of water into the air as water vapor and back to Earth's surface as precipitation (prih sihp-uh TAY shuhn). **Precipitation** is any form of water that falls from clouds to Earth.

WATER CYCLE Water moves into the air as a gas. It then falls back to Earth as a liquid.

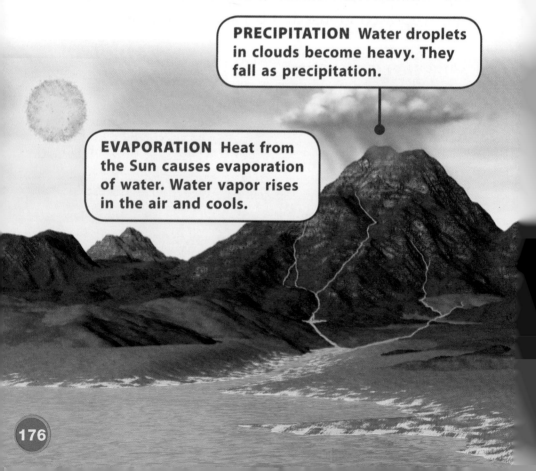

PRECIPITATION Water droplets in clouds become heavy. They fall as precipitation.

EVAPORATION Heat from the Sun causes evaporation of water. Water vapor rises in the air and cools.

Water in oceans, lakes, and rivers evaporates and becomes water vapor. As water vapor rises in the air, it cools and condenses into water droplets. These droplets form clouds. As more water vapor condenses, the drops become heavier and heavier. They become so heavy, they fall to Earth as precipitation.

Some precipitation flows downhill on Earth's surface. This water is called runoff. Runoff water flows toward streams, rivers, lakes, and oceans. Some precipitation flows down into the ground. This water is called groundwater.

CONDENSATION Cooled water vapor condenses into water droplets. These form clouds.

Types of Clouds

Clouds form when water vapor in the air condenses. A cloud that forms close to the ground is called fog.

Stratus (STRAT uhs) clouds are low-level clouds that form in layers. Stratus clouds usually bring rain.

Cumulus (KYOOM yoo luhs) clouds are fluffy and are flat at the bottom. They form low in the sky. They usually mean fair weather.

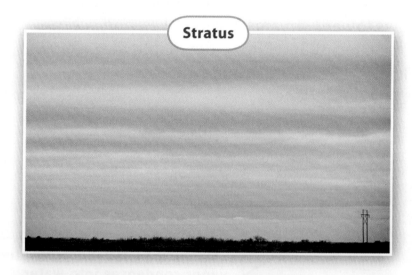

Stratus

Cumulus

Cirrus (SEER uhs) clouds are thin clouds that look like feathers. They are made of ice crystals. They form high in the sky. Cirrus clouds mean the weather is fair.

Cumulonimbus (kyoom yoo lo NIHM buhs) clouds bring thunderstorms.

Cirrus

Cumulonimbus

Forms of Precipitation

Precipitation is any form of water that falls from clouds. Rain, snow, sleet, and hail are all forms of precipitation.

Rain is the most common form of precipitation. It rains when drops of water fall through air that is above freezing.

Sleet is rain that freezes as it falls. If the temperature near Earth's surface is below freezing, rain turns to ice before it reaches the ground.

Rain is falling drops of liquid water.

Sleet forms when rain freezes as it falls.

Snow falls when the temperature in a cloud is below freezing. Water vapor in the cloud forms ice crystals. These ice crystals are called snowflakes.

Hail forms when drops of rain freeze and strong winds carry them higher into a cloud. As hailstones fall again, more ice forms on them. They become larger. This can happen over and over. Finally, the hailstones are too heavy to be lifted by the wind. Then they fall to Earth.

Snow is falling ice crystals.

A hailstone can be as big as a baseball.

SEQUENCE

Describe the stages in the water cycle.

3   What Causes Weather?

Scientists gather information about temperature, water vapor, wind, and air pressure. They use this information to try to guess what the weather will do.

Weather Conditions

Weather is all the conditions of the atmosphere at a certain time and place. These conditions include temperature, amount of water vapor in the air, wind, and air pressure.

The temperature is how hot or cold the air is. The amount of water vapor in the air is called humidity (hyoo MIHD uh tee). High humidity can make the air feel wet and sticky. Wind is the movement of air. As you know, air pressure is the weight of air as it presses down on Earth.

Weather is the conditions of the atmosphere at a certain time and place.

Each weather condition can be measured using a different tool.

A rain gauge collects and measures the amount of precipitation that has fallen in an area.

A thermometer measures the temperature of the air.

An anemometer (an uh MAHM uh tuhr) measures the speed of the wind.

A barometer (buh RAH muh tur) measures air pressure.

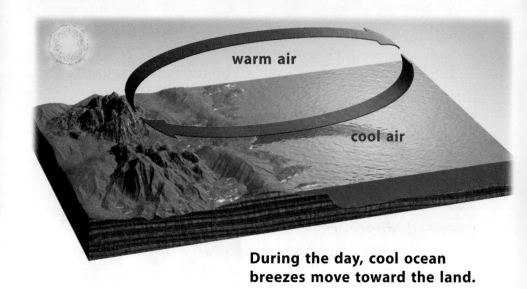

warm air

cool air

During the day, cool ocean breezes move toward the land.

Wind

Wind is moving air. Air flows from places of high pressure to places of low pressure.

During the day, Earth's surfaces take in heat from the Sun. The land becomes warm quickly. It warms the air above it. As the air warms, it rises. This causes a spot of low pressure.

Oceans warm slowly. During the day, air above the ocean is not as warm as air over land. This cooler air does not rise. It stays close to Earth's surface. This causes a spot of high pressure.

As the warm air above the land rises, the cooler air above the ocean moves in to take its place. This flow of air, or wind, is called a sea breeze.

Air Masses

Each place on Earth warms or cools the air above it. This creates an air mass. An **air mass** is a large body of air that has about the same temperature, air pressure, and moisture.

Two conditions are used to describe air masses—temperature and humidity. Air masses are either warm or cold, and they are either moist or dry. Air masses that form in warm places are usually warm. Air masses that form near cold places are cold. Air masses that form over oceans are moist. Those over land are usually dry.

Most changes in weather happen when one air mass moves into a place and pushes out another air mass.

The arrows show the movement of air masses that affect the United States.

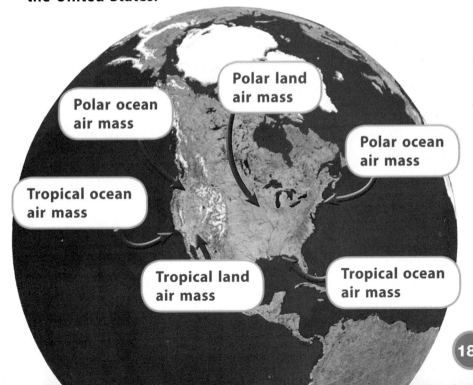

Polar land air mass

Polar ocean air mass

Polar ocean air mass

Tropical ocean air mass

Tropical land air mass

Tropical ocean air mass

Weather Patterns

Air masses do not stay in one place. As they move, they bump into each other. The place where two air masses meet is called a **front**. A front moves across Earth's surface as one air mass pushes against the other. The weather can change suddenly when a front moves across an area. Most storms and precipitation take place along fronts.

A cold front forms as a cold air mass meets a warm air mass. The cold air moves under the warm air, pushing it up. As the warm air rises, clouds form and precipitation occurs. Thunderstorms often happen along a cold front.

A cold front can cause a line of powerful thunderstorms that moves across the United States.

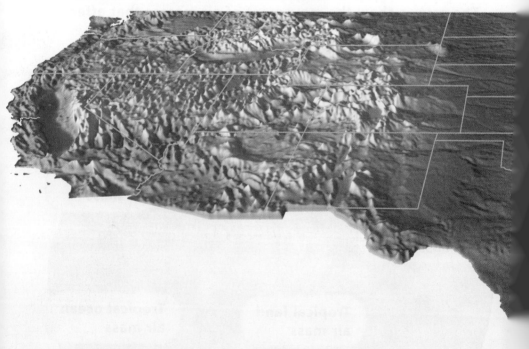

A warm front forms as a warm air mass pushes into a cold air mass. The warm air slowly moves up over the cold air. Layers of gray clouds and steady precipitation are seen when a warm front moves into an area.

The same types of air masses usually form over North America each year. The air masses usually move in the same direction, too. This creates weather patterns that repeat with the seasons. For example, a cold air mass moves down from Canada. A warm air mass moves up from Mexico. These air masses sometimes push against each other. The cold front can cause violent thunderstorms and tornadoes.

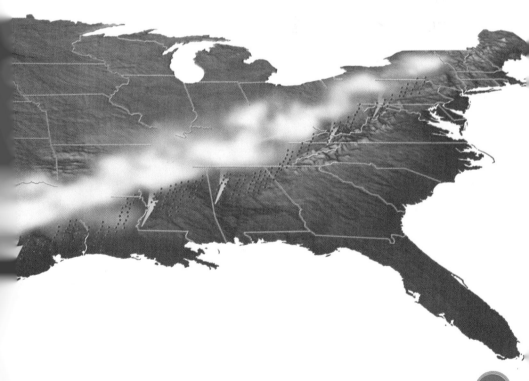

Analyzing Weather Data

A meteorologist (mee tee uh RAHL uh jihst) is a scientist who studies weather. Studying weather involves measuring conditions near Earth's surface and high in the atmosphere.

Meteorologists use these measurements to identify the kinds of air masses over an area. They also predict what kind of front will form and where that front will move. This is used to create a weather map. Weather maps are often used as part of a weather forecast. A forecast is a prediction of what the weather will be for a certain day, week, or longer period of time.

Weather maps use symbols to show the location of fronts and precipitation.

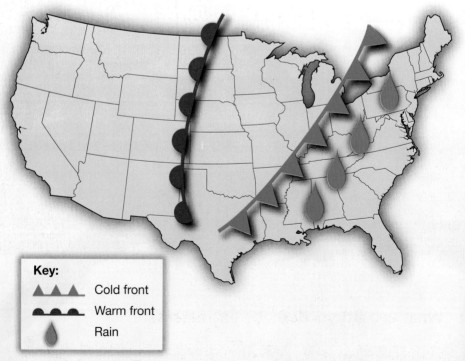

Key:
▲▲▲ Cold front
●●● Warm front
🌢 Rain

Severe Weather

Severe weather includes hurricanes, tornadoes, and snowstorms. Hurricanes often cause floods and strong winds. Severe storms, including hurricanes and blizzards, can destroy homes and put people in harm's way.

Meteorologists study storms using tools that are in space and on the ground. Forecasters give weather warnings when severe weather is likely to move into an area. These warnings can save lives. They give people time to prepare for the storm. Warnings also give people time to leave an area that it in the path of severe weather.

A hurricane is a huge swirling storm that forms over the ocean.

MAIN IDEA AND DETAILS

What conditions describe air masses?

4 How Does Climate Change?

Climate is the usual weather conditions of a place. Climate is different in different areas of the world.

Major Climate Zones

If someone asked you what winter is like in your area, you could not say exactly what the temperature would be or how much snow or rain would fall on a certain day. But you could give a general idea of what the weather would be during winter. In other words, you could describe your climate (KLY muht). **Climate** is the usual weather conditions in an area over time. The climate of an area has a lot to do with the kinds of plants and animals that can live there.

Tropical fish can only survive in hot climates where the water is warm.

Climate Zones

Polar climate

Tropical climate

Temperate climate

Equator

Key:
Polar
Temperate
Tropical

Earth is divided into three climate zones. The warmest climates are found in the tropical climate zone. A **tropical climate** is hot and rainy. The tropical climate zone is near the equator. The equator is an imaginary line around Earth. It gets strong sunlight all year.

The coldest climate zones are the areas around the North and South Pole. The poles get the least amount of sunlight on Earth. A **polar climate** has very cold temperatures year round.

Most of the United States is in a temperate (TEHM pur iht) zone. The temperate zones are between the tropical and polar zones. A **temperate climate** often has warm, dry summers and cold, wet winters.

Factors Affecting Climate

The amount of sunlight an area gets affects its climate. How much sunlight an area gets depends on its latitude (LAT ih tood), or its distance north or south of the equator. Low latitudes are near the equator. The Sun is high in the sky and the temperature is hot.

High latitudes are farther from the equator. Sunlight strikes the surface at an angle. The temperature is colder.

Oceans and other bodies of water also affect climate. A large body of water usually causes the climate to be wet and mild.

OREGON
Oregon is at high latitude. But the ocean warms the coast.

MAINE
Maine is at a northern latitude. It has cold, snowy winters.

45°
40°
35°
30°
25°

FLORIDA
Florida is at a low latitude. Its climate is warm.

Altitude (AL tih tood), or height above sea level, also affects climate. The higher you travel up a mountain, the colder it gets.

Mountains can affect climate in other ways. Mountains can block the path of air masses. When a warm, wet air mass reaches a mountain, the air mass is forced upward. The air mass cools as it rises. The water vapor in the air mass condenses. It then falls on the mountain as precipitation.

When the air mass moves over the mountain, the air is dry. The land on the other side of the mountain might get so little precipitation that it is a desert.

The Alps are a group of high mountains. The tops are cold and snowy. The climate at the bottom is fairly mild.

How Climates Have Changed

The climate where you live has likely been the same for many years. But climates do not stay the same forever. They can change both in certain spots and over the whole Earth.

Much of North America was covered by ice about 20,000 years ago. This period of time is called the ice age. Since the ice age, Earth's climate has become warmer. Many scientists think that Earth's climate may still be warming.

Scientists think Earth's atmosphere has been damaged by some chemicals humans use. The damaged parts, shown in purple in this picture, allow harmful rays from the Sun to reach Earth's surface. This may be one reason why Earth's climate is warming.

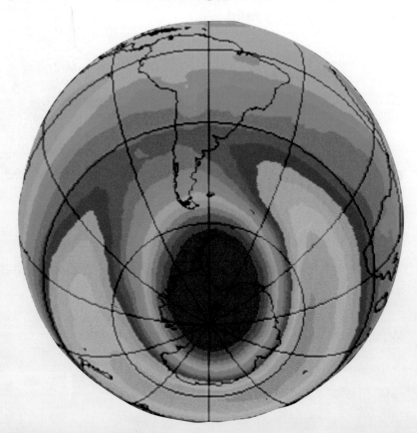

Scientists learn about climate in different ways. They look at tree rings in very old fossils to learn what the climate was like when the tree was alive. Scientists have also taken core samples of ice from Antarctica, at the South Pole. This ice can be hundreds of years old. Each layer holds traces of air from long ago. These ice core samples have helped scientists understand how climates have changed.

Each layer of an ice core holds bits of dust, gases, and other things. Scientists can tell what the atmosphere was like in the past by studying ice cores.

CAUSE AND EFFECT

What causes a polar climate to be so cold?

Glossary

air mass (air mas) A large body of air that has about the same temperature, air pressure, and moisture throughout.

air pressure (air PRESH uhr) The weight of air as it presses down on Earth's surface.

atmosphere (AT muh sfihr) The layers of air that surround Earth's surface.

climate (KLY muht) The average weather conditions in an area over a long period of time.

condensation (kahn dehn SAY shuhn) The change of the state of gas to a liquid.

evaporation (ih vap uh RAY shuhn) The change of state from a liquid to a gas.

front (fruhnt) The place where two air masses meet.

greenhouse effect (GREEN hows ih FEHKT) The process by which heat from the Sun builds up near Earth's surface and is trapped there by the atmosphere.

Glossary

polar climate (POH lur KLY muht) Places with polar climate have very cold temperatures throughout the year, and are located around the North Pole and the South Pole.

precipitation (prih sihp ih TAY shuhn) Any form of water that falls from clouds to Earth's surface.

temperate climate (TEHM pur iht KLY muht) Places with temperate climate usually have warm, dry summers and cold, wet winters.

tropical climate (TRAHP ih kuhl KLY miht) Places with tropical climate are hot and rainy for most of or all of the year.

water cycle (WAH tur SY kuhl) The movement of water into the air as water vapor and back to Earth's surface as precipitation.

weather (WEHTH ur) The conditions of the atmosphere at a certain place and time.

Responding

Think About What You Have Read

Vocabulary

❶ The usual weather conditions in an area over a long period of time is _____ .

A) climate

B) weather

C) greenhouse effect

D) season

Comprehension

❷ What are the two main gases in air? What helped you find the answer?

❸ What causes clouds to form? What step in the water cycle comes before this process?

❹ What are three factors that affect climate?

Critical Thinking

❺ How would you describe the climate in your area? How might the latitude, landforms, bodies of water, and air masses of your area affect your climate?

Looking at the Universe

Contents

How Is the Sun Important to Earth?

The Sun gives off energy that helps keep life going on Earth.

Energy from the Sun

Energy from the Sun warms Earth's land and water. But land and water heat up at different speeds. Water warms more slowly than sand and soil do. This means that oceans, lakes, and other bodies of water warm more slowly than the land near them.

These differences cause wind. Earth's surface is heated and warms the air above it. Some places on Earth are heated more than others. So the air above these places is warmed more. The warmer air rises. Cooler air moves in to take its place. This movement of air is wind.

The Sun warms Earth. In this picture, they are shown much closer together than they really are.

Earth

Sun

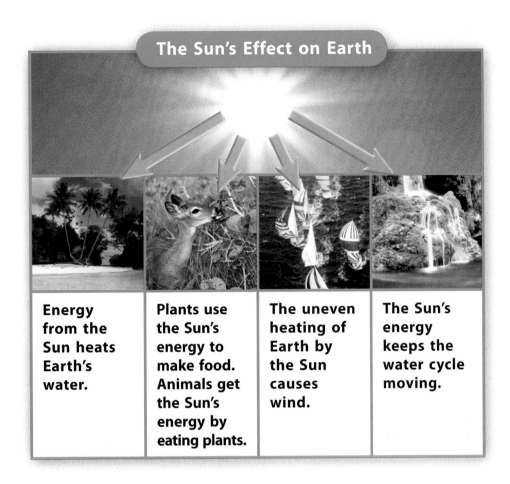

The Sun's Effect on Earth

Energy from the Sun heats Earth's water.	Plants use the Sun's energy to make food. Animals get the Sun's energy by eating plants.	The uneven heating of Earth by the Sun causes wind.	The Sun's energy keeps the water cycle moving.

Energy from the Sun keeps water moving through the water cycle. When the Sun heats water on Earth's surface, some of the water moves into the air as water vapor. Clouds form when the water vapor cools and turns into tiny drops of water. When the drops become too heavy for the cloud to hold, they fall to Earth as rain.

The Sun gives plants energy to make food. Green plants use the energy in sunlight to make food. In this way, a plant stores the Sun's energy. When an animal eats the plant, some of that stored energy is passed on to the animal.

The Sun and Solar System

The Sun makes its own light. Earth and the Moon do not make their own light. Moonlight is light from the Sun that bounces off the Moon.

Earth is a **planet**, or large body made of rock or gas that moves around a star. Earth's path as it travels around the Sun is called its **orbit** (AWR biht). A moon is a body that moves in an orbit around a planet.

The Sun is at the center of the solar system (SOH lur SIHS tuhm). The **solar system** is made up of the Sun, eight major planets, many dwarf planets, and other smaller bodies that orbit the Sun.

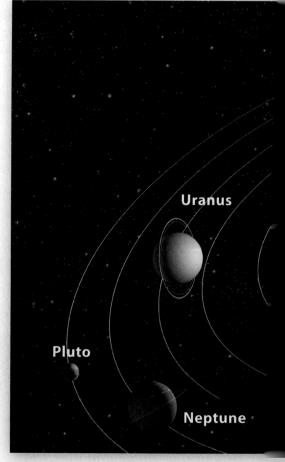

Uranus

Pluto

Neptune

The Sun is at the center of the solar system.

Comparing the Sun, Earth, and Moon

Body	Surface
Sun	Very hot gases on the Sun's surface are always moving.
Earth	Earth's surface is covered mostly by water, rock, and soil.
Moon	The Moon's surface is dry and dusty. It has mountains and craters but no atmosphere.

Gravity

Gravity (GRAV ih tee) is the force that pulls bodies or objects toward other bodies or objects. When you jump up, gravity pulls you back toward Earth. Gravity also keeps the planets orbiting the Sun.

The Sun, the planets, and the Moon all have gravity. They pull on each other. But they pull with different amounts of force. The amount of gravity that a body has depends on its mass.

The mass of Earth is greater than the mass of the Moon. So Earth's gravity is stronger than the Moon's. You would weigh less on the Moon than you do on Earth. You could also jump higher on the Moon than on Earth.

A lot of force is needed to overcome the pull of Earth's gravity and lift the space shuttle into space.

DRAW CONCLUSIONS

Why would an astronaut be able to lift heavy things more easily on the Moon than on Earth?

2 What Are the Outer Planets?

The planets farthest from the Sun are called the outer planets.

Comparing Planets

Earth, Mercury, Venus, and Mars are the four planets closest to the Sun. They are called the inner planets. The inner planets are smaller than the other planets in the solar system. While the inner planets are made of materials that are alike, they are not exactly the same.

The major planets farthest from the Sun are the outer planets. They are very different from the inner planets. Jupiter, Saturn, Uranus, and Neptune are often called the **gas giants**. They are the largest planets in the solar system and are made mostly of gas.

Mercury	Venus	Mars
	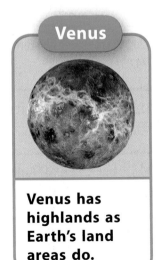	
Mercury has many craters.	Venus has highlands as Earth's land areas do.	Mars is the planet most like Earth.

Inner and Outer Planets

Inner Planets

Planet (in order from Sun)	Diameter	Mass (compared with Earth)	Rings or Moons
Mercury	4,879 km (3,032 miles)	0.06 of Earth's mass	None
Venus	12,104 km (7,521 miles)	0.82 of Earth's mass	None
Earth	12,756 km (7,926 miles)	1 Earth	1 Moon
Mars	6,794 km (4,222 miles)	0.11 of Earth's mass	2 Moons

Outer Planets

Planet (in order from Sun)	Diameter	Mass (compared with Earth)	Rings or Moons
Jupiter	142,980 km (88,846 miles)	318 Earths	Rings Many moons
Saturn	120,540 km (74,897 miles)	95 Earths	Rings Many moons
Uranus	51,120 km (31,763 miles)	15 Earths	Rings Many moons
Neptune	49,530 km (30,775 miles)	17 Earths	Rings Many moons
Pluto (dwarf planet)	2,390 km (1,485 miles)	less than 0.005 Earth's	Moons

Jupiter

Jupiter is the largest planet. In fact, more than 1,000 Earths would fit inside Jupiter. It is so big that all the other planets would fit inside it! A huge storm in Jupiter's atmosphere, called the Great Red Spot, is more than twice the size of Earth.

Like other gas giants, Jupiter is made up mostly of gases. It is covered by a very deep atmosphere that has high and low clouds. These clouds change color each day. They move in bands in opposite directions. Jupiter has at least 63 moons. Scientists think the planet probably has even more moons than this.

Four of Jupiter's moons can be seen through binoculars.

Saturn is so light that it could float on water.

Saturn

Saturn has bright, beautiful rings. They are made of pieces of ice, dust, and rocks. Most of these pieces are only a few centimeters (about an inch) across. Some are as large as a house. Together the rings are about 282,000 kilometers (175 miles) wide, but they are very thin.

Saturn is the second largest planet. Like the other gas giants, it is covered by clouds. It also has a small but thick rocky center. Saturn has many moons.

Uranus

Uranus is the third largest planet. It is only one-third the size of Jupiter. As many as 64 Earths would fit into Uranus. Methane, a gas in Uranus's atmosphere, gives the planet its beautiful blue-green color.

Uranus has rings. They are very hard to see. Scientists did not even know they were there until 1977. Most were found in 1986. Uranus also has many moons. You can see Uranus in the sky with binoculars. But you have to know exactly where to look.

Uranus seems to rotate on its side.

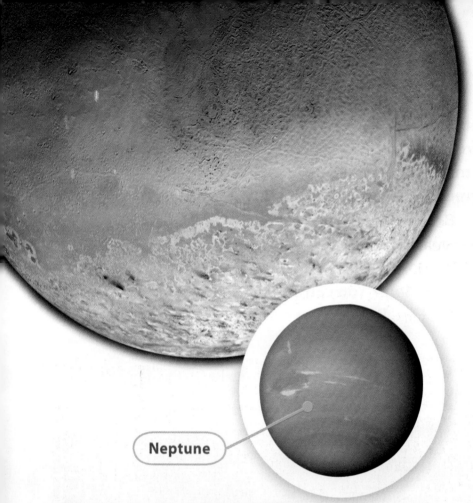

Neptune

Triton is Neptune's largest moon.

Neptune

Neptune is the fourth largest planet in the solar system. It is the smallest of the four gas giants. While it is a bit smaller than Uranus, Neptune has a greater mass. Neptune is almost 5 billion kilometers (about 3 billion miles) from the Sun.

Neptune has fewer moons than the other gas giants. It has a very busy atmosphere. The winds here are very strong, and the planet has huge storms.

Pluto

Pluto is different from all the other major planets. It is a dwarf planet. It is smaller than Neptune's largest moon! Pluto is not a gas giant. It is rocky and icy.

Pluto's orbit has a greater oval shape and is tilted compared with the orbits of other planets.

Because Pluto is so different, scientists discussed for years whether or not it really was a planet. In 2006 scientists classified Pluto as a dwarf planet because Pluto is so much smaller than the other major planets.

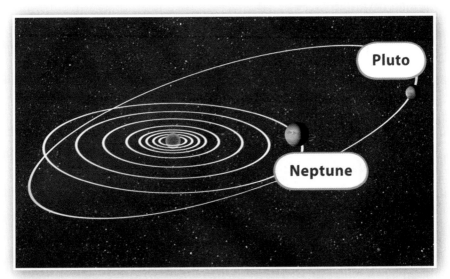

Pluto's orbit is an extreme oval and is tilted.

COMPARE AND CONTRAST

Tell how Jupiter and Pluto are alike and different. Record your ideas in a Venn diagram.

3 How Do Earth and Its Moon Move?

When Earth and the Moon move, it causes many changes. It causes changes in seasons, daylight hours, the phases of the Moon, and the night sky.

How Earth Moves

Earth makes one complete trip around the Sun in a year. While orbiting the Sun, Earth also turns on an imaginary line called an **axis** (AK sihs). With each **rotation** (roh TAY shuhn), or turn, on Earth's axis, there is one period of daylight and one period of night. Earth's axis is tilted slightly from its orbit. This tilt and Earth's orbit around the Sun cause Earth's seasons.

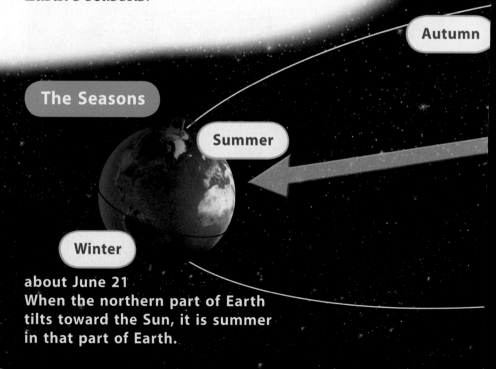

The Seasons

Autumn

Summer

Winter

about June 21
When the northern part of Earth tilts toward the Sun, it is summer in that part of Earth.

As Earth orbits the Sun, different parts of it are tilted toward the Sun. When the northern half of Earth tilts toward the Sun, it is summer there. Sunlight hits that part of Earth more directly. The air is warmer. The period of daylight is longer.

When the northern half of Earth tilts away from the Sun, it is winter there. Sunlight hits that part of Earth less directly. The air is colder. The period of daylight is shorter.

Because Earth's axis is tilted, parts of Earth have four different seasons.

Spring

about March 21
The northern part of Earth begins tilting toward the Sun.

Winter

Summer

about December 22
When the northern part of Earth tilts away from the Sun, it is winter in that part of Earth.

Autumn

about September 23
The northern part of Earth has stopped tilting toward the Sun. It will begin to point away from the Sun.

Spring

How the Moon Moves

When you look at the Moon, you always see the same craters and mountains. You see the same things because the same side of the Moon always faces Earth.

Why does the same side of the Moon always face Earth? Like Earth, the Moon rotates on its axis. The Moon rotates once every 27.3 days. The Moon also orbits Earth once every 27.3 days. Because these two things take the same amount of time, the same side of the Moon always faces Earth.

Half of the Moon is always lighted by sunlight. But as the Moon orbits Earth, the amount of the lighted side facing Earth changes. These changes cause the phases of the Moon.

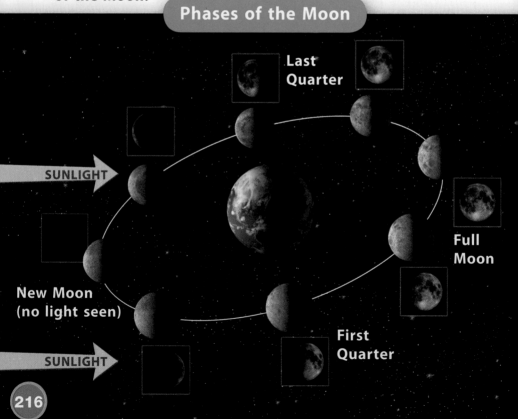

Phases of the Moon

Last Quarter

SUNLIGHT

Full Moon

New Moon (no light seen)

First Quarter

SUNLIGHT

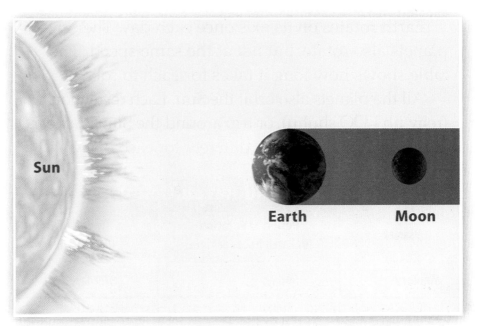

Sun

Earth

Moon

Earth blocks light from the Sun during a lunar eclipse. The Moon is in Earth's shadow.

You have probably noticed that the Moon seems to change shape from one night to the next. Why? Recall that the Moon does not make its own light. It reflects, or sends back, light from the Sun.

Half of the Moon is almost always in sunlight. As the Moon orbits Earth, the amount of the lighted side facing Earth changes. These changes cause **phases of the Moon**.

The Moon is not lighted by sunlight during a lunar eclipse (LOO nur ih KLIHPS). A **lunar eclipse** occurs when the Moon passes into Earth's shadow. This happens two to four times a year.

Comparing Planet Movements

Earth rotates on its axis once each day. The other planets also rotate, but not at the same speed. The table shows how long it takes for each to rotate.

All the planets also orbit the Sun. Each **revolution** (rehv uh LOO shuhn), or trip around the Sun, is a year. But the length of a year is different for each planet.

Rotation and Revolution

Planet	Period of Rotation (in Earth hours or time)	Period of Revolution
Mercury	59 days	87.9 days
Venus	243 days	225 days
Earth	23 hours, 56 minutes	365.25 days
Mars	25 hours	1.88 years
Jupiter	9 hours, 55 minutes	11.86 years
Saturn	10 hours, 40 minutes	29.46 years
Uranus	17 hours, 14 minutes	84 years
Neptune	16 hours, 6 minutes	164.79 years
Pluto (dwarf)	6 days, 15 minutes	248.54 years

CAUSE AND EFFECT

Why do people on Earth always see the same side of the Moon?

4 What Are Stars and Galaxies?

The universe is made up of all the stars, galaxies, planets, and moons in space.

The Suns and Other Stars

A **star** is a huge ball of very hot gases. It gives off light, heat, and other kinds of energy. Stars can be grouped by their size, color, brightness, and temperature.

The Sun is a star. It is medium in size and brightness. Many other stars are larger and brighter. Why does the Sun look so much brighter than any other star? The reason is that the Sun is much closer to Earth than any other star.

The Sun's energy has been giving Earth light and heat for 4.5 billion years.

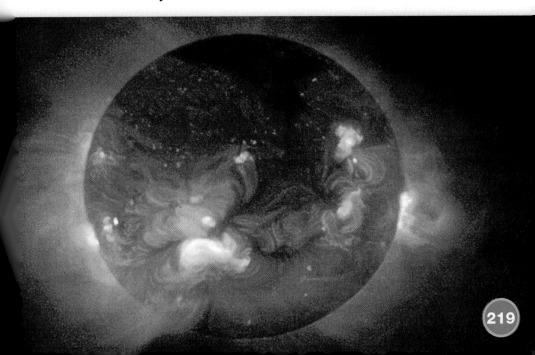

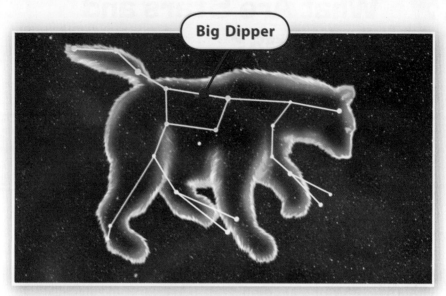

Ursa Major is a constellation. People long ago thought this group of stars looked like a bear.

Constellations

A **constellation** (KAHN stuh lay shuhn) is a group of stars that forms a pattern in the night sky. One well-known constellation is called Ursa Major (UR suh MAY jur), which means "Great Bear." Some of the stars in Ursa Major make up another group of stars called the Big Dipper.

Have you ever looked at a bright star early in the evening? If you look for it again later that night, it will be in a different spot. The stars do not actually move, however. They seem to move because Earth is rotating. As Earth rotates on its axis, you see different parts of the sky.

Galaxies

The Sun, the planets, and the moons are part of the solar system. The solar system is part of a larger group, too. It is part of a galaxy (GAL uhk see). A **galaxy** is a huge system, or group, of stars held together by gravity. The solar system is in a galaxy called the Milky Way.

The **universe** (YOO nuh vurs) is made up of all the matter and energy there is. This includes all the galaxies and their stars, planets, and moons. There are billions of galaxies in the universe. No one knows how big the universe is. Scientists think it is growing even bigger.

Milky Way Galaxy

Location of Solar System

The stars and planets that you see at night are in the Milky Way Galaxy.

MAIN IDEA AND DETAILS

What is a galaxy?

axis (AK sihs) An imaginary line through the center of an object.

constellation (KAHN stuh lay shuhn) A group of stars that forms a pattern in the night sky.

galaxy (GAL uhk see) A huge system, or group, of stars held together by gravity.

gas giants (gas JY hunts) The four largest planets in Earth's solar system—Jupiter, Saturn, Uranus, and Neptune—that consist mainly of gases.

gravity (GRAV ih tee) The force that pulls bodies or objects toward other bodies or objects.

lunar eclipse (LOO nur ih KLIHPS) An event in which the Moon passes into Earth's shadow.

orbit (AWR biht) The path that Earth and the other planets make as they move around the Sun.

Glossary

phases of the Moon (FAYZ ihz uhv thuh moon) Changes in the amount of the sunlit half of the Moon that can be seen from Earth.

planet (PLAN iht) A large body of rock or gas that does not produce its own light and orbits around a star.

revolution (rehv uh LOO shuhn) The movement in a path around an object, as when the Earth travels around the Sun; one complete trip around the Sun.

rotation (roh TAY shuhn) The turning of a planet on its axis.

solar system (SOH lur SIHS tuhm) A system made up of the Sun, eight major planets, many dwarf planets, and smaller bodies that orbit the Sun.

star (stahr) A huge ball of very hot gases that gives off light, heat, and other kinds of energy.

universe (YOO nuh vurs) The system made up of all the matter and energy there is, including the galaxies, and their stars, planets, and moons.

Think About What You Have Read

Vocabulary

❶ Earth travels around the Sun along a path called a/an _____ .

A) rotation

B) orbit

C) eclipse

D) axis

Comprehension

❷ How does the Sun support life on Earth?

❸ List the outer planets in order from nearest to farthest from the Sun.

❹ The Sun shines more directly in the northern part of Earth during which season?

Critical Thinking

❺ How are the solar system, the Milky Way, and the universe related?

Managing Earth's Resources

Contents

1

What Are Renewable Resources?

Earth has many things that people need and use. Many of these things can be replaced.

Air and Water

A **natural resource** (NACH ur uhl REE sawrs) is a material found on Earth that can be used by people. Trees, soil, and minerals are a few natural resources.

Some natural resources, such as oil, are nonrenewable (nahn rih NOO uh buhl). A **nonrenewable resource** is one that cannot be replaced once it is used up or that takes thousands of years to be replaced.

A **renewable resource** (rih NOO uh buhl) is a natural resource that can be replaced or can replace or renew itself. Air and water are renewable resources that all living things need.

Plants and Animals

Plants and animals are renewable resources. Animals get energy by eating plants or by eating other animals that eat plants.

Plants help clean and renew the air. Plants make their own food. As they do this, they take in a gas called carbon dioxide. They also let go of a gas called oxygen. Animals breathe oxygen from the air. Without plants, the animals would use up all the oxygen.

When old plants die, new plants often grow in their place naturally. People can help new plants grow by farming. After a food crop is picked, a new crop can be planted.

Soil, plants, trees, and water are renewable resources.

People use the wood from trees. Wood is used to make things like buildings, chairs, and paper.

Some plants can be used to help people who are hurt or sick. There is a gel inside the leaves of the aloe vera (AL oh VEHR uh) plant. The gel can help heal cuts or burns.

People use animals in many ways. One important way that people use animals is as food.

People use wood from trees to make things, such as paper.

Water as a Resource

All living things need water to live. But most of Earth's water is found in oceans. Most plants and animals cannot use this water. It has too much salt in it.

Only a small amount of Earth's water is fresh water. Most of the fresh water is under the ground or is trapped in glaciers and ice caps. Less than 1 percent of Earth's water is found in rivers and lakes. It is this water that is used for drinking and washing.

The water cycle is the way nature renews the supply of fresh water. In this cycle, energy from the Sun heats Earth's water. The heat changes the water into a gas called water vapor. The process in which liquid water changes to water vapor is called **evaporation** (ih vap uh RAY shuhn). When water evaporates, anything that is mixed with the water is left behind.

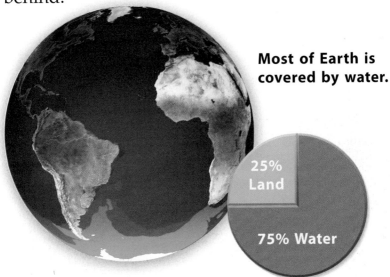

Most of Earth is covered by water.

25% Land

75% Water

When water vapor cools, it forms tiny drops of liquid water. **Condensation** (kahn dehn SAY shuhn) is the process in which water vapor turns back into liquid water. This happens when water vapor rises to the upper parts of air. Air is colder higher up than it is near land.

Clouds are made when drops of water form around small particles in the air. When the drops become too heavy, they fall from the clouds as rain, snow, sleet, or hail.

Water that falls to Earth is called **precipitation** (prih sihp ih TAY shuhn). Precipitation returns fresh water to Earth. Some of it flows into the ground. The rest of it flows into oceans, lakes, and rivers. The water cycle repeats again and again.

The water you drink today is the same water that was on Earth millions of years ago.

Uses of Water

Water runs downhill from mountains into rivers, lakes, and reservoirs (REHZ uhr vwahrz). Reservoirs are natural lakes or lakes made by people. Water is saved in reservoirs for farms, homes, and businesses to use.

Firefighters use water to save lives and buildings.

Boats let people use water as a way to travel and to have fun.

Farmers use water to grow crops.

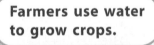

All living things need fresh water.

Soil and Nutrients

Soil is an important resource. Most plants need soil to grow. Soil gives the plants support and nutrients. If the soil used for growing crops is well cared for, it can be used again and again.

Some crops use a lot of nutrients as they grow. If a farmer plants the same crop in the same soil every year, it uses up some of the nutrients. Some crops help put nutrients back into the soil. Many farmers change the crops they grow. One time they will grow a crop that uses up nutrients. The next time they will grow a crop that gives back those nutrients.

Fertilizers (FUR tl eye zurz) are chemicals. Farmers add these to the soil to give back lost nutrients. Some fertilizers come from nature. Others are made in factories.

2

What Are Nonrenewable Resources?

Some natural resources are nonrenewable.
The fossil fuels and minerals found in Earth's crust
are nonrenewable resources.

Fossil Fuels

People use energy every day. They use it to run
their lights and computers. They use it to heat and
cool their homes, schools, and businesses. A small
amount of energy comes from renewable resources.
These resources include the Sun, wind, moving
water, and heat from inside Earth.

However, most of the energy used in the United
States comes from nonrenewable resources called
fossil fuels (FAHS uhl FYOO uhlz). A **fossil fuel** is
made from the remains of ancient plants and
animals. Fossil fuels are oil, natural gas, and coal.
These fuels began forming on Earth more than
300 million years ago.

We get some coal from strip mines, like this one.

Coal

Coal is the most common fossil fuel on Earth. The energy stored in coal is used mainly to make electricity. It is also used for heating. A type of coal called coke is used to make iron and steel.

How Coal Forms

PEAT
Long ago swamp plants died and were covered with rock and soil.

LIGNITE
(LIHG nyt) Layers of rock, soil, and water covered the peat. Then heat from below and pressure from above changed the peat into lignite.

BITUMINOUS
(bih TOO muh nuhs) More heat and pressure makes bituminous coal.

ANTHRACITE
(AN thruh syt) More heat and pressure turns bituminous coal into anthracite.

Oil and Natural Gas

Oil and natural gas are also fossil fuels. They are formed much like coal. But instead of swamp plants, they are made from animals and plants that lived in Earth's oceans. Over millions of years, heat and pressure changed the remains of these plants and animals into oil. More heat and pressure changed some oil into natural gas.

Oil is used as fuel for cars and trucks. It is also used to make things like plastics, medicines, and cloth.

Natural gas is used to heat many homes and businesses. It is also used to run some machines, such as stoves.

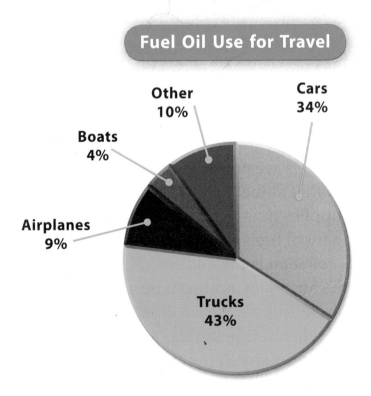

Fuel Oil Use for Travel

Other 10%
Cars 34%
Boats 4%
Airplanes 9%
Trucks 43%

Using fossil fuels can make air pollution.

Fossil Fuels — Pro and Con

As sources of energy, there are some good things about fossil fuels. They are fairly easy to get out of the ground. They are easy to move from place to place. They are often cheaper than other forms of energy. There are enough supplies now to meet people's needs.

There are also some problems with using fossil fuels. All fossil fuels are nonrenewable. Some scientists think that at the rate oil and natural gas are used today, supplies may run out in 100 years.

Also, using fossil fuels makes pollution (puh LOO shuhn). **Pollution** is the adding of harmful materials to the air, water, and soil. Burning fossil fuels causes air pollution.

Oil can spill when it is being moved from place to place. This can hurt many living things. They may become sick or die when they touch the spilled oil.

Some people do not want to use fossil fuels. They want to use renewable energy sources. These sources include power from sunlight and wind. They also include hydroelectric (HY droh ih LEHK trihk) power, which is energy that comes from moving water.

These energy sources will not run out and they do not produce pollution. But they can cost a lot. Scientists are working to find ways to make renewable energy sources cheaper and easier to use. The first car you own might run on water!

This woman is working with solar energy panels. The panels make power from sunlight.

Layers of Soil

Soil is made up in part of tiny pieces of rock. The process of making soil takes a long time. In fact, the top inch of soil in most places started forming about 500 years ago.

Nutrients lost from soil can be replaced. This means soil can be thought of as a renewable resource. But some soil is lost because of erosion. When this happens, it takes a long time to be replaced. That is why soil can be thought of as nonrenewable.

Rich soil contains humus (HYOO muhs) and minerals. **Humus** is a material made up of decayed plants and animal matter. Rich soil is good for growing most plants.

A **soil profile** (soyl PROH fyl) is a cross section of soil that shows the different layers in soil. Soil profiles are different from place to place. Most of the time, a profile has four layers. These layers are called horizons (huh RY zuhnz).

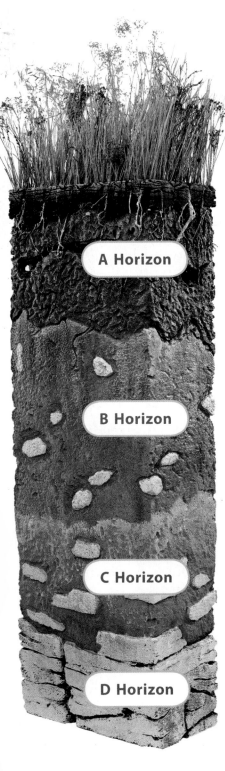

A Horizon

A HORIZON: This layer is topsoil (TAHP soyl), the upper layer of soil that contains minerals and humus.

B Horizon

B HORIZON: This layer contains minerals but very little humus.

C Horizon

C HORIZON: This layer is mostly broken up, weathered rocks.

D Horizon

D HORIZON: This layer is bedrock, the solid rock below the lowest layer of soil.

Types of Soils

Soils are grouped by the type of rock bits that are in them. The three main types are sand, silt, and clay. Water drains quickly through sandy soils. Pieces of silt are smaller than sand particles. Most silt floats on top of water.

Clay has the smallest pieces. Water puddles form on top of clay because the tiny pieces are packed so tightly together.

Most plants have a hard time growing in soil made of only one of these types. But plants grow very well in loam (lohm). Loam is a made up of humus, sand, silt, and clay. Loams have different amounts of these materials. Different plants, trees, and crops grow in different soil types.

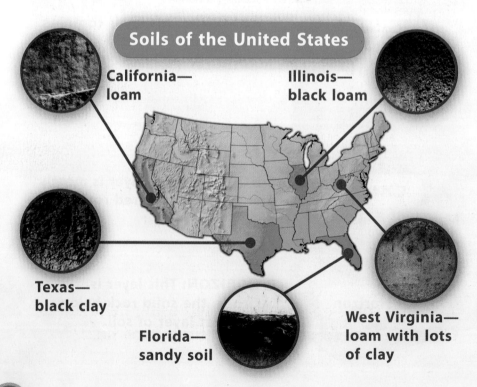

Soils of the United States

California—
loam

Illinois—
black loam

Texas—
black clay

Florida—
sandy soil

West Virginia—
loam with lots
of clay

Rocks and Minerals

Everything on Earth that is not living or has never lived is made from minerals. Living things need minerals to grow and stay healthy.

Remember that rock is a solid material that is made up of one or more minerals. Rocks are always changing very slowly in the rock cycle. People mine minerals, such as iron and copper. Over time, these minerals will be replaced in the rock cycle.

But the rock cycle is very slow. Plus, some minerals are rare, which means there are not a lot of them. That is why minerals are thought of as nonrenewable resources.

Many minerals are used to make buildings.

COMPARE AND CONTRAST

What are some good things about using fossil fuels? What are some problems with using fossil fuels?

3

How Can Resources Be Conserved?

There are many things people can do to protect Earth's natural resources and the environment.

Tons of Garbage

People throw away lots of things, such as paper towels and plastic bottles. Many of the items that are thrown away make life easier. But some of the materials used to make them are pollutants (puh LOOT uhnts). A **pollutant** is a material that causes pollution.

Millions of tons of garbage are thrown away each year. Much of it ends up in places called landfills. Pollutants in landfills can make their way into the ground and into lakes and rivers.

This garbage is being put into a landfill.

Good and Bad Practices

In the United States, there are laws that make companies and the places people live control pollution. There are also laws that support the act of conservation (kahn sur VAY shuhn). **Conservation** is the preserving and wise use of natural resources.

Some laws tell companies to clean up pollution they cause. Other laws tell which chemicals may or may not be safely let go into the environment (ehn VY ruhn muhnt). An environment is everything that surrounds and affects living things.

All these laws help protect natural resources. But more laws are needed.

Garbage by Percent

7% Food

16% Yard Waste

37% Paper and Cardboard

29% Wood, Plastic, Metal, and Glass

11% Other

Reduce, Reuse, Recycle

You help to conserve Earth's natural resources by practicing the three R's of conservation — reduce, reuse, and recycle. There are different ways to reduce and reuse. For example, using cloth bags to carry groceries can reduce, or make less, the number of plastic or paper bags thrown away. You can also reduce waste by buying products that use less packaging.

You can help reduce the number of new products that need to be made. One way to do this is to sell used items or give them to charity.

Another good practice is to use products that are biodegradable (by oh dih GRAY duh buhl). A **biodegradable** product is one that breaks down easily in the environment. Tissues are an example of a biodegradable product.

This house is made of recycled cans.

Recycling is important to conservation. Most towns have recycling programs that gather used items made from certain materials. Things that can be recycled include newspapers, cans, and some plastics.

Think about why it is important to recycle an aluminum can. Aluminum ore is a nonrenewable resource. It takes energy to mine and process the ore. It takes more energy to make the can. It takes less energy to make a new can using recycled aluminum. Recycling aluminum helps conserve an important resource.

Plastic and paper products can be recycled. Many things, such as cloth and furniture, are made from recycled products.

Earth's resources will last much longer if everyone reduces, reuses, and recycles.

This fleece is made from recycled plastic bottles.

This backpack is made from recycled plastic bottles.

PROBLEM AND SOLUTION

What are some ways to conserve natural resources?

Glossary

biodegradable (by oh dih GRAY duh buhl) Able to break down easily in the environment.

condensation (kahn dehn SAY shuhn) The change of the state of gas to a liquid.

conservation (kahn sur VAY shuhn) The preserving and wise use of natural resources.

evaporation (ih vap uh RAY shuhn) The change of state from a liquid to a gas.

fossil fuel (FAHS uhl FYOO uhl) A fuel that formed from the remains of ancient plants and animals.

humus (HYOO muhs) A material made up of decayed plant and animal matter.

natural resource (NACH ur uhl REE sawrs) A material on Earth that is useful to people.

nonrenewable resource (nahn rih NOO uh buhl REE sawrs) A natural resource that cannot be replaced once it is used up or that takes thousands of years to be replaced.

Glossary

pollutant (puh LOOT uhnt) Any harmful material added to the air, the water, and the soil.

pollution (puh LOO shuhn) The addition of harmful materials to the air, the water, and the soil.

precipitation (prih sihp ih TAY shuhn) Any form of water that falls from clouds to Earth's surface.

renewable resource (rih NOO uh buhl REE sawrs) A natural resource that can be replaced or can replace or renew itself.

soil profile (soyl PROH fyl) A lengthwise cross section of soil that shows the different layers.

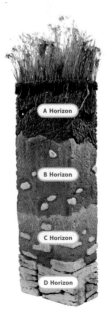

A Horizon

B Horizon

C Horizon

D Horizon

topsoil (TAHP soyl) The upper layer of soil that contains minerals and humus.

Responding

Think About What You Have Read

Vocabulary

❶ One renewable natural resource is _____ .

A) natural gas

B) copper

C) air

D) plastic

Comprehension

❷ What is a renewable resource?

❸ Why are fossil fuels and minerals nonrenewable resources?

❹ What are some ways that Earth's resources can be conserved?

Critical Thinking

❺ Based on what you have learned, how could you change your own ways of living to help conserve natural resources?

Life Cycles

Contents

How Do Plant Life Cycles Vary?

Flowering plants make seeds during their life cycles. The seeds grow into new plants. Plants live for different lengths of time.

Life Cycle of a Flowering Plant

A small seed is planted in the ground. The seed grows into a tall tree. The tree flowers and makes its own seeds. One day the tree dies. This is the life cycle of a tree.

A **life cycle** (lyf SY kuhl) is the series of changes that happen during a lifetime. The changes in a life cycle include birth, becoming an adult, reproduction, and death.

Flowering plants grow flowers during their life cycles. Flowers make seeds that will grow into new plants. Some flowering plants include trees and grasses.

Life Cycle of a Flowering Plant

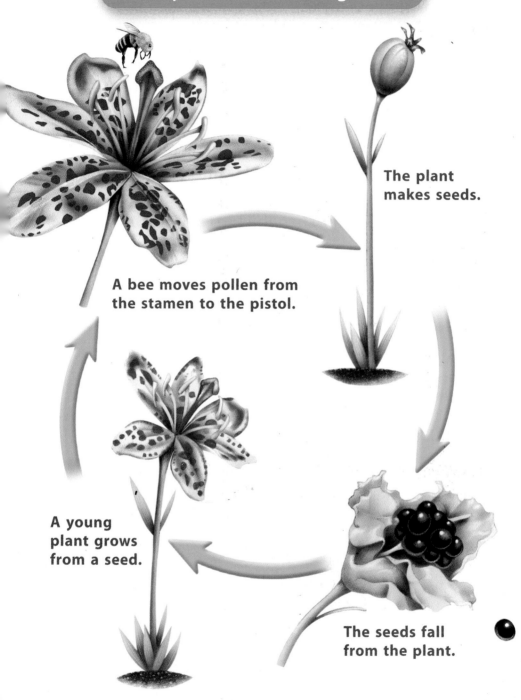

A bee moves pollen from the stamen to the pistol.

The plant makes seeds.

A young plant grows from a seed.

The seeds fall from the plant.

The stamen (STAY muhn) of a flower makes pollen. Flowers make seeds when pollen is moved from the stamens to the pistil (PIHS tuhl). Wind, water, and animals can move pollen.

Each seed holds an embryo. An **embryo** (EHM bree oh) is a plant or animal in the earliest stages of development.

Some seeds will fall in places where they can germinate. To **germinate** (JUHR muh nayt) means to begin growing a new plant. The new plant grows and forms flowers. Then the life cycle begins again.

PISTIL
When pollen is moved from the stamens to the pistil, the flower makes seeds.

STAMENS
The stamens make pollen.

Life Spans of Plants

A **life span** is the length of time it takes a living thing to complete its life cycle. The length of a life span is different for different kinds of plants. Bean seeds will grow into plants, make seeds, and die in one summer. A maple tree may live for hundreds of years.

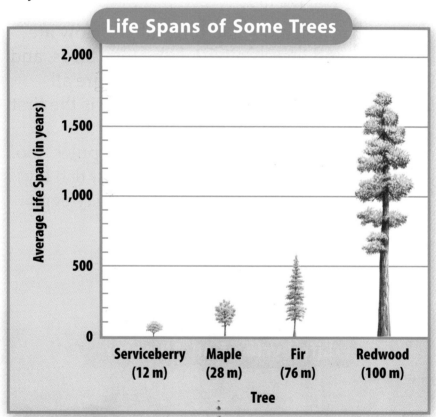

Life Spans of Some Trees

Average Life Span (in years)

2,000 · 1,500 · 1,000 · 500 · 0

Serviceberry (12 m) · Maple (28 m) · Fir (76 m) · Redwood (100 m)

Tree

SEQUENCE

What step in the plant life cycle comes after pollen is moved?

2 How Do Animal Life Cycles Vary?

All animals have life cycles during which they grow and reproduce. Animals live for different lengths of time.

Metamorphosis

How are alligators and birds alike? How are alligators and insects alike? Alligators, birds, and insects do not look the same, but they are all animals. They also all lay eggs. An **egg** is the first stage in the life cycle of most animals.

Alligators are reptiles. Snakes are reptiles, too. All reptiles lay eggs. All birds and most fish lay eggs. Most amphibians, such as frogs, lay eggs. Even insects lay eggs.

Life Cycle of an Alligator

Different types of animals lay different numbers of eggs. An eagle may lay 2 or 3 eggs at a time. Some frogs lay thousands of eggs. An ocean sunfish can lay around 300 million eggs at one time.

Offspring hatch from eggs. An offspring is a new living thing born when parents reproduce. An offspring grows into an adult. An **adult** is a fully-grown organism.

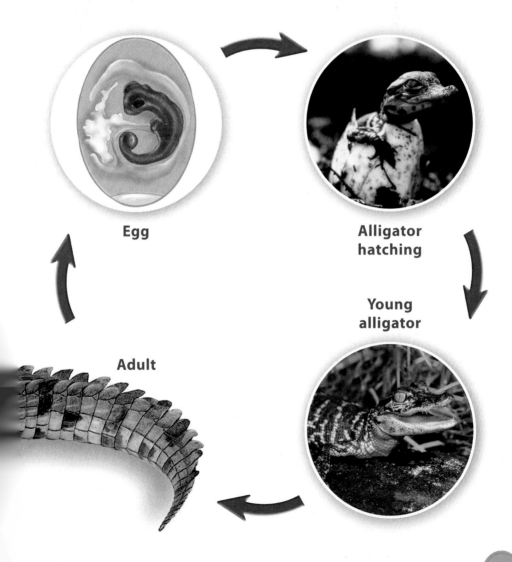

Egg

Alligator hatching

Young alligator

Adult

Life Cycle of a Mexican Bean Beetle

Larva

Egg

Some living things change form in different stages of their life cycles. This process of change is called **metamorphosis** (meht uh MAWR fuh sihs). Many insects change form four times. This is called complete metamorphosis.

The egg is the first stage. The egg hatches into a wormlike form called a **larva** (LAHR vuh). The larva is the second stage. The larva eats and grows larger.

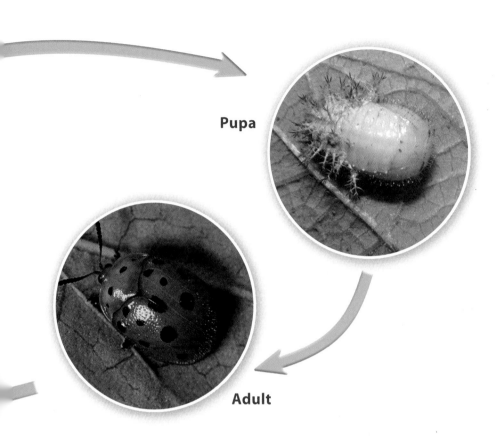

Pupa

Adult

    In the third stage, the larva forms a hard shell around itself. This is called the pupa (PYOO puh). In the fourth stage, the adult insect comes out of the pupa. The insect looks very different at each stage.

    Some insects change form only three times. This is called incomplete metamorphosis. The egg is the first stage. The **nymph** (nihmf) is the second stage. The nymph looks like the adult without wings. The nymph will get bigger, grow wings, and become an adult. The adult is the third stage.

Life Cycles and Life Spans

Many animals lay eggs during their life cycles. For example, baby birds hatch from eggs. The babies grow and become adults. To reproduce, adult female birds lay eggs. In time, the adult birds die.

Rabbits, bears, and humans are mammals. Mammals do not lay eggs. Their young are born live. Like baby birds, young mammals grow and become adults. The adults reproduce and in time die.

A life span is the length of time it takes a living thing to complete a life cycle. Different kinds of animals have different life spans.

Bird egg

Smaller animals usually have shorter life spans than larger animals of the same kind. For example, lizards and alligators are both reptiles. A small lizard may live only 2 years, but an alligator can live 60 years. This is not always true, however. Humans and elephants are both mammals. Humans are much smaller than elephants but can live longer.

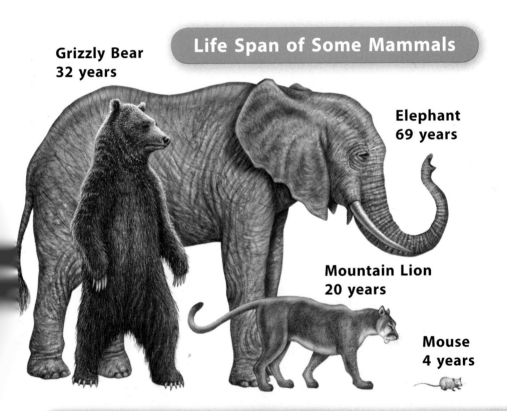

**Grizzly Bear
32 years**

Life Span of Some Mammals

**Elephant
69 years**

**Mountain Lion
20 years**

**Mouse
4 years**

COMPARE AND CONTRAST

How do mammals and birds differ in the way they produce young?

How Are Offspring Like Their Parents?

Living things look like their parents because they inherit their parents' traits. Some living things look different when they are young but grow to look like their parents.

Look Alikes

A young polar bear looks like an adult polar bear. Young living things grow to look like their parents. A duckling will grow to look like its parents. It will not look like an eagle. Apple seeds grow into apple trees. They do not grow to look like pine trees.

Features such as color and shape are examples of traits. A **trait** (trayt) is a feature of a living thing. Traits of humans include eye color and hair color. Other traits include the shape of the eye, nose, and mouth.

Traits of birds include the color of feathers and the shape of the beak. Traits of plants include the color of flowers and the shape of the leaves. Traits of insects include the color of the body and number of wings.

Young organisms usually **inherit** (ihn HEHR iht) many traits from their parents. A child with curly hair usually has a parent with curly hair.

Inherited Traits

An inherited trait is a trait that is passed from parents to offspring. A plant inherits the shape of its leaves. Some inherited traits may change slightly. A bird may have a little longer beak than its parents. However, the parents and offspring still look alike.

Living things with two parents inherit traits from both parents. A child may have curly hair like her father and blue eyes like her mother.

Not all living things look like their parents at birth. For example, tadpoles do not look like adult frogs. A tadpole has to go through metamorphosis. Then it begins to look like its parents.

The tadpole and an adult frog look very different.

MAIN IDEA

Why might an adult animal not look exactly like its parents?

Glossary

adult (uh DUHLT)
A fully-grown, mature organism.

egg (ehg) The first stage in the life cycle of most animals.

embryo (EHM bree oh) A plant or animal in the earliest stages of development.

germinate (JUHR muh nayt) The process in which a seed begins to grow into a new plant.

inherit (ihn HEHR iht) To receive traits from parents.

Glossary

larva (LAHR vuh) The wormlike form that hatches from an egg. The second stage of an organism that goes through complete metamorphosis.

life cycle (lyf SY kuhl) A series of stages that occur during the lifetimes of all organisms.

life span (lyf span) The length of time it takes for an individual organism to complete its life cycle.

metamorphosis (meht uh MAWR fuh sihs) The process in which some organisms change form in different stages of their life cycles.

trait (trayt) A feature or characteristic of a living thing.

Responding

Think About What You Have Read

Vocabulary

1 Which would not be an inherited trait?

A) brown eyes

B) straight hair

C) leaf shape

D) speaking French

Comprehension

2 What are the main stages in the life cycle of a flowering plant?

3 How is the life cycle of a rabbit different from the life cycle of a bird?

4 How are complete and incomplete metamorphosis alike and different?

Critical Thinking

5 "Offspring look exactly like their parents." Is this statement accurate? Explain your answer.

Responses
of Living
Things

Contents

1

How Do Living Things Learn About Their World?

Living things sense and respond to changes in their environment. Living things respond to things from outside their bodies and from inside their bodies.

Using the Senses

All living things respond to their surroundings, or environment (ehn VY ruhn muhnt). The **environment** is everything that surrounds a living thing.

How do you learn about your environment? You use sense organs such as your eyes, nose, ears, and skin. You use your eyes to see and your nose to smell. You use your ears to hear and your skin to touch. Special parts of your tongue help you taste the food you eat.

The doctor uses special drops to look in eyes. The drops make the pupils larger.

Pupil before drops.

Pupil after drops.

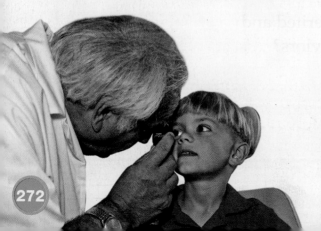

Imagine that you feel a cold wind. How would you respond? You might shiver and put on a sweater. The cold wind is a stimulus (STIHM yuh luhs). A **stimulus** is anything that causes a living thing to react. A reaction to a stimulus is called a **response** (rih SPAHNS). Shivering and putting on a sweater are responses.

Like you, many animals use their senses to learn about their environment. They often use their good senses of smell and hearing to observe stimuli (STIHM yuh ly) and respond.

Plants do not have five senses, but they do respond to stimuli. Plants grow toward light. Many plants sag when they need water.

The moose uses its good sense of smell to find food.

Other Sense Organs

Some people think bats are blind. That is not true. Bats can see, but most do not see well. They use another sense to find food. Some bats like to eat moths. To find them, the bats send out sound waves. The sound waves bounce off objects and go back to the bats. This is called echolocation. Dolphins also use echolocation.

Bats do not always catch the moths. Many moths have sense organs that pick up the bat's sound waves. When a moth senses a bat, it tries to get away. It may fly away, fly in loops, or drop to the ground and hide.

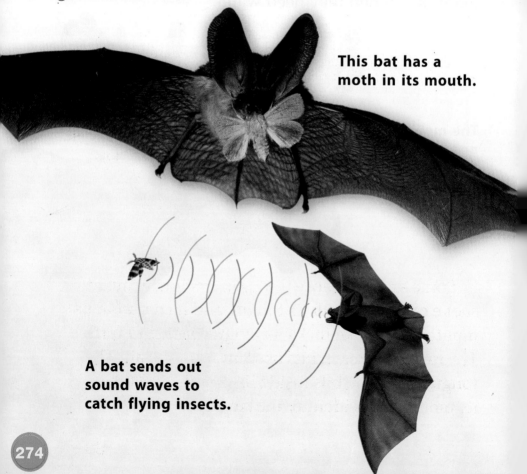

This bat has a moth in its mouth.

A bat sends out sound waves to catch flying insects.

A snake's tongue helps it smell.

Some animals sense things in unusual ways. A snake can smell with its tongue and an organ in its mouth. The snake flicks its tongue back and forth. The tongue takes in bits of scent from the air. The tongue takes the bits inside its mouth. The organ in its mouth helps identify the smell.

External and Internal Stimuli

Living things respond to things from outside their bodies and from inside their bodies. The word external means from the outside. The word internal means from the inside.

Anything in the environment that causes a living thing to respond is an **external stimulus** (ihk STUR nuhl STIHM yuh luhs). Bright sunlight is an external stimulus for most plants. The plants grow toward the light. Sound waves from a bat are external stimuli for a moth.

An **internal stimulus** (ihn TUR nuhl STIHM yuh luhs) is anything within a living thing that causes it to respond. Hunger pains are an internal stimulus. The response is to eat.

A kingfisher responds to hunger by diving for a fish. This is an example of an internal stimulus.

A morning glory vine wraps itself around a pole. This is another example of an internal stimulus.

Plants and animals respond to both external and internal stimuli. Some dogs respond to the sight and sound of a can of dog food being opened. The sight of the can and the sound of it being opened are external stimuli.

As a morning glory vine grows, it searches for something to climb. An internal stimulus causes the stem of the plant to grow up around a pole.

CAUSE AND EFFECT

Give an example of an internal stimulus and a response to that stimulus.

2 What Are Inherited and Learned Behaviors?

Living things are born with some behaviors. They learn other behaviors.

Inherited Behavior

A bird flies south for the winter. A baby sea turtle crawls toward the ocean. You comb your hair. These are behaviors (bih HAYV yuhrz) in living things. The way that a living thing acts or responds to its environment is its **behavior**.

Many behaviors must be learned. Other behaviors are inherited. An **inherited behavior** is one that a living thing is born with and does not learn. A reflex is a simple inherited behavior. It is not learned. When the doctor taps your knee, your leg kicks out. That is a reflex.

Baby sea turtles crawl toward the ocean. This is an inherited behavior.

A complex pattern of behavior that living things of the same type are born with is called an **instinct** (IHN stihngkt). Orb spiders are born with an instinct to make a certain kind of web. Each spider knows how to make the web without being taught how.

This orb spider is making a web. This behavior is called an instinct.

All grosbeak weaver birds build nests like this one. This behavior is also called an instinct.

All grosbeak weaver birds build the same kind of nest. Each bird knows how to make the nest without being taught how. This behavior is another example of an instinct.

Many birds move to another place when the weather gets colder. The birds are born with this instinct to migrate (MY grayt). Many whales, fish, and insects also migrate.

Some animals go into a deep sleep during winter. The animals are born with this instinct to hibernate (HY bur nayt). They sleep through the winter when there is little food. They wake in the spring when there is more food.

Learned Behavior

Think of something you enjoy doing. Perhaps you like to play soccer. Maybe you enjoy bike riding. Someone probably taught you how to do this. Or, you may have learned by watching others. A behavior that is taught to you is a **learned behavior**.

People are not the only animals that learn behaviors. Chimpanzees learn from each other. One behavior chimpanzees learn is to use sticks to get termites to eat. Animals also learn from experience. For example, rats learn how to avoid traps in their search for food.

Chimpanzees use sticks to eat termites. This is a learned behavior.

sea otter

Learning new behaviors can help animals survive. Animals can learn new behaviors when things change around them. Sea otters use rocks to crack open shells. They eat what is inside. Sometimes people throw bottles in the sea. Some sea otters learn to use old bottles to crack open shells.

Young children and animals learn many behaviors from adults. How did you learn to read? How did you learn to write? You probably learned these behaviors from adults. How does a young tiger learn to hunt? It learns by watching adult tigers.

Grooming is a learned behavior. Young monkeys learn how to groom from adults.

Sometimes people teach animals how to do things. People train animals by giving commands and rewarding the correct behavior. For example, dogs can be trained to sit and stay. Training must be repeated many times.

Most animals learn behaviors when they are young. It may be more difficult to learn as they get older. However, some people learn new things late in life. Some people in their 80s have gotten college degrees.

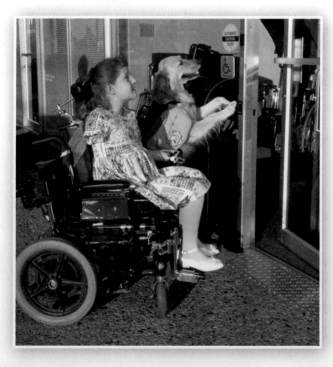

Some dogs can be trained to help people.

DRAW CONCLUSIONS

What learned behaviors help an animal survive?

Glossary

behavior (bih HAYV yur) The way that an organism acts or responds to its environment.

environment (ehn VY ruhn muhnt) Everything that surrounds and affects a living thing.

external stimulus (ihk STUR nuhl STIHM yuh luhs) Anything in an organism's environment that causes it to react.

inherited behavior (ihn HEHR iht uhd bih HAYV yur) A behavior that an organism is born with and does not need to learn.

instinct (IHN stihngkt) A complex pattern of behavior that organisms of the same type are born with.

internal stimulus (ihn TUR nuhl STIHM yuh luhs) Anything within an organism that causes it to react.

learned behavior (lurnd bih HAYV yur) A behavior that is taught or learned from experience.

response (rih SPAHNS) A reaction to a stimulus.

stimulus (STIHM yuh luhs) Anything that causes a living thing to react.

Responding

Think About What You Have Read

Vocabulary

1 After hearing a loud sound, you cover your ears. The sound is a/an _____ .

    A) internal stimulus

    B) external stimulus

    C) inherited behavior

    D) learned behavior

Comprehension

2 How does hibernating help animals survive?

3 What do organisms use to learn about their environment?

4 Identify the two main types of behavior.

Critical Thinking

5 Do you think that two different kinds of birds that live in different environments would make the same kind of nest? Why or why not?

Parts of Ecosystems

Contents

What Are Nonliving Parts of Ecosystems?

Nonliving parts of an ecosystem include water, air, and sunlight. Living things need these nonliving things.

Ecosystems and Nonliving Things

Plants and animals are living things. To live and grow, plants and animals need nonliving things. Nonliving things include water, air, and light. An **ecosystem** (EE koh sihs tuhm) is made up of all the living and nonliving things that interact in an area.

Soil is a nonliving thing. Plants grow in soil. **Soil** is another word for dirt and is made up of tiny pieces of rock and organic (awr GAN ihk) matter. **Organic matter** is the remains of plants and animals. It is rich in nutrients. Nutrients are materials that help living things grow.

Both plants and animals need sunlight. Plants need sunlight to make food. Some plants and animals can live only where it is warm. Others grow better in the shade of trees.

A Forest Ecosystem

LIGHT
Plants need light
to make food.

AIR
Plants and animals
need air.

WATER
A stream provides
water.

SHADE
Some living things grow
better in shade.

SOIL
Soil provides plants with
support and nutrients.

Different Ecosystems

Each ecosystem is different. The nonliving parts of each are different. The nonliving parts include light, water, temperature, and soil. Only some living things can live in each ecosystem. A living thing can only live where its needs are met.

A Polar Ecosystem There is no soil in a polar ecosystem. There is only ice. Temperatures are very cold. There is little or no sunlight for about half the year. Some animals do live in a polar ecosystem. Polar bears can live there. Polar bears have thick fur to keep warm. The bears hunt and eat animals that live in the ocean water.

A Desert Ecosystem It is very hot during the day in a desert ecosystem. There is very little rain in a desert. The soil is sandy. It has few nutrients. Some plants and animals do live in a desert. They make changes to live here. Desert plants send roots deep into the ground to find water. Desert animals look for food at night when it is cooler.

CLASSIFY

What are some nonliving parts of an ecosystem?

2 What Are Living Parts of Ecosystems?

Different ecosystems are home to different kinds of living things.

Communities and Populations

You know that an ecosystem is made up of all the living and nonliving things in an area. A forest ecosystem has many kinds of living things. Many kinds of plants and animals can find the things they need to live in a forest.

A living thing can live only in an environment (ehn VY ruhn muhnt) that meets its needs. An **environment** is everything that surrounds and affects a living thing.

All the living things in an ecosystem make up a **community** (kuh MYOO nih tee). A community is made up of different populations (pahp yuh LAY shunz) of living things. A **population** is all the members of one kind of plant or animal. For example, all the beavers in a forest are one population.

294

A Forest Ecosystem

Birds use trees for shelter.

Deer use grass and leaves for food.

Beavers use trees to build a shelter.

Trillium plants grow in shady areas.

The Right Ecosystem

In a **rainforest** (RAYN fawr ist), it rains a lot. Many rainforests are warm all year. There is a rainforest in Washington State. The temperatures of this rainforest are mild. Trees grow close together. This rainforest provides shelter and water for many kinds of animals.

A **prairie** (PRAIR ee) is a grassy area with few or no trees. Prairies get more rain than deserts, but less than forests. Winters are cold, and summers are hot. The prairie is home to animals that eat grasses and their seeds.

Some Ecosystems in the United States

WASHINGTON

SOUTH DAKOTA

rainforest

prairie

There are ecosystems in cities. New York City's Central Park is home for many plants and animals. New York City is in a temperate (TEHM pur iht) zone. A **temperate zone** is an area that rarely gets very hot or very cold.

The Florida Everglades is an ecosystem. Most of the land is covered by water. Some trees and tall grasses grow from the muddy water. Water plants and animals such as shrimp and fish live in the water.

Conditions vary in different parts of each ecosystem. Plants and animals live where the conditions are right for them.

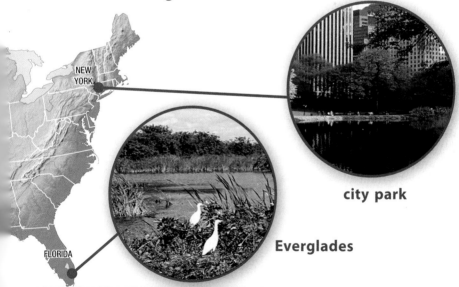

NEW YORK

FLORIDA

city park

Everglades

CAUSE AND EFFECT

Explain why forest ecosystems support so many kinds of plants and animals.

3 What Are Some Roles of Living Things?

Living things in an ecosystem depend on one another. They help one another meet needs such as food, shelter, and protection.

Interdependence

Living things in an ecosystem depend on each other to meet their needs. They are interdependent (ihn tur dih PEHN duhnt). You know that many animals depend on plants for food. Plants provide food and shelter for some animals. In turn, the animals can provide protection for the plant.

The swollen thorn acacia tree and a type of stinging ant are interdependent. The ants live in the tree. They eat a sugary liquid in the tree's leaves. The ants help the tree by protecting it. When another kind of animal starts eating the tree, many ants sting the animal. The ants drive the animal away.

Stinging ants live in the swollen thorn acacia tree.

Another example of interdependence occurs in Africa. The Nile crocodile and a bird called the Egyptian plover help each other. The crocodile lets the bird come into its mouth. There the bird eats little animals on the crocodile's gums. Both animals benefit. The bird gets a meal. The crocodile gets its teeth cleaned.

The Egyptian plover cleans the crocodile's teeth. The bird gets a meal.

Relationships in an Ecosystem

Every living thing has a role to play, or a job to do. Plants play the role of producer (pruh DOO sur). A **producer** is a living thing that makes its own food.

Plants use energy from sunlight to make food. Plants use energy from the food they make to grow. Some of the food is stored in the leaves, stem, and roots.

When an animal eats a plant, energy in the plant moves into the animal. Animals are consumers (kuhn SOO murz). A **consumer** gets energy by eating plants, or by eating other animals that eat plants. All consumers in some way depend on producers for food.

The kapok tree provides shelter.

scarlet macaws

tapir

Shelter is another basic need of living things. The need for shelter is often met with the help of other living things. For example, squirrels and many kinds of birds make their homes in trees.

Trees provide shelter for plants, too. Ferns and mosses might grow in the shade of a tree.

Some animals provide shelter for other animals. Woodchucks dig tunnels underground. They live there for some time and then move on. Other animals such as skunks and rabbits may live in the tunnels next.

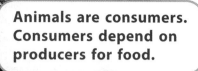

ferns

Pollinators and Seed Dispersal

Some living things help other living things carry out reproduction (ree pruh DUHK shuhn). **Reproduction** is the process of making more of one's own kind.

Many plants reproduce by making seeds. For a plant to make seeds, pollen (PAHL uhn) must move from one part of a flower to another part, or from one flower to another flower. How does pollen move? Wind and water can carry pollen. Animals such as insects and birds can carry pollen, too. An animal that helps plants make seeds is called a **pollinator** (PAHL uh nay tur).

Pollinators feed on pollen. They carry pollen from flower to flower. When pollen touches the right part of the flower, seeds begin to form.

Some plants depend on animals to carry their seeds to new places. **Seed dispersal** (dih SPUR suhl) is the scattering or carrying away of seeds from the plant. Some plant seeds get caught in the fur of animals. These seeds may be carried a long way before falling off.

Some plants grow fruit. Seeds form inside the fruit. Animals eat the fruit. They drop the seeds or leave them in their waste. If the seeds fall where conditions are right, the seeds will grow.

MAIN IDEA

How do plants depend on animals to reproduce?

Glossary

community (kuh MYOO nih tee) All the organisms that live in the same ecosystem and interact with each other.

consumer (kuhn SOO mur) An organism that eats other living things to get energy.

ecosystem (EE koh SIHS tuhm) All living and nonliving things that exist and interact in one place.

environment (ehn VY ruhn muhnt) Everything that surrounds and affects a living thing.

organic matter (awr GAN ihk MAT ur) The remains of plants and animals.

pollinator (PAHL uh nay tur) An animal, such as an insect or bird, that helps plants make seeds by moving pollen from one part of the plant to another.

population (pahp yuh LAY shun) All the organisms of the same kind that live in an ecosystem.

Glossary

prairie (PRAIR ee) A grassy land area with few or no trees.

producer (pruh DOO sur) Any organism that makes its own food.

rainforest (RAYN fawr ihst) An area with a great deal of rainfall. Most rainforests are warm all year, and there is a lot of sunlight.

reproduction (ree pruh DUHK shun) The process of making more of one's own kind.

seed dispersal (seed dih SPUR suhl) The scattering or carrying away of seeds from the plant that produced them.

soil (soyl) The loose material that covers much of Earth's surface.

temperate zone (TEHM pur iht zohn) An area of Earth where the temperature rarely gets very hot or very cold. The temperate zones are located between the tropical zone and the polar zones.

Think About What You Have Read

Vocabulary

❶ Everything that surrounds and affects a living thing is called its _____ .

A) environment

B) temperate zone

C) population

D) prairie

Comprehension

❷ How do nonliving parts of an ecosystem help a plant or animal meet its needs?

❸ What might happen if all the trees in a forest ecosystem were cut down?

❹ Name two ways that an animal might depend on a plant.

Critical Thinking

❹ Explain the difference between an ecosystem and a community.

Matter and Energy in Ecosystems

Contents

How Does Energy Flow in a Food Web?

Energy flows from the Sun to producers. Then energy flows from producers to consumers.

Energy from the Sun

All living things need energy to stay alive. They get that energy from food.

Plants do not eat food. Plants are producers. Producers are living things that make their own food. The way most plants make food is called **photosynthesis** (foh toh SIHN thih sihs). This takes place in a plant's leaves. Light energy from the Sun is trapped inside the leaves. Plants use light energy and carbon dioxide gas from the air to make food.

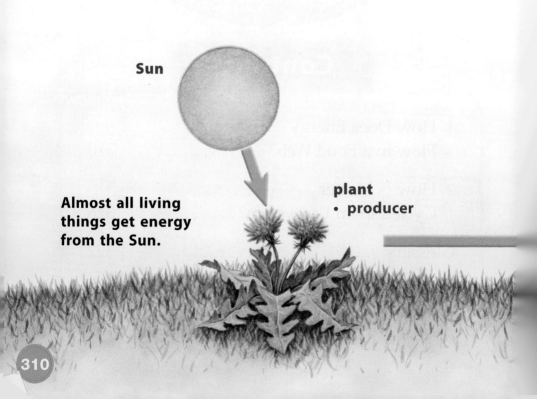

Sun

plant
• producer

Almost all living things get energy from the Sun.

Predator and Prey

Animals are consumers. Consumers are living things that eat other living things. Some animals eat plants. Some animals eat other animals that eat plants. A **predator** (PREHD uh tawr) is an animal that hunts other animals for food. **Prey** (pray) is an animal that is hunted for food by another animal.

The picture shows how energy flows from the Sun to plants. A consumer, such as a rabbit, eats a plant. The rabbit receives some of the plant's energy. A predator, such as a fox, eats the rabbit. The fox receives a smaller amount of the plant's energy.

Energy flows from the Sun to a producer, and then to consumers. Energy flows from prey to predator.

fox
- consumer
- predator

rabbit
- consumer
- prey

plant
• producer

This food chain has four steps.

vole
• consumer
• herbivore
• prey

Food Chains

A **food chain** shows the path of food energy in an ecosystem. Remember that an ecosystem is all living and nonliving things that interact in one place. A food chain begins with producers. Plants are producers. Plants use photosynthesis and energy from the Sun to make food.

Consumers are also part of the food chain. There are three kinds of consumers. An **herbivore** (HUR buh vawr) is an animal that eats only plants. An **omnivore** (AHM nuh vawr) is an animal that eats both plants and animals. A **carnivore** (KAHR nuh vawr) is an animal that only eats other animals.

An herbivore gets energy from eating plants. An omnivore gets energy from eating plants and animals. A carnivore gets energy from eating animals.

skunk
- consumer
- omnivore

owl
- consumer
- carnivore
- predator

The pictures show a forest food chain. The plant makes its own food. An herbivore, such as a vole, eats the plant. An omnivore, such as a skunk, eats the vole. Finally, a carnivore, such as an owl, eats the skunk.

At each step in the food chain, some of the energy is lost. For example, the plant does not keep all of the food it makes. It uses some energy to grow flowers and seeds for the plant.

The vole gets only some of the plant's energy. The vole uses some of that energy to run from its predators. The skunk gets less energy from eating the vole. There is less energy available at each step in a food chain. That is why most food chains only have four or five steps.

Food Webs

Most ecosystems have many different kinds of plants and animals. Each plant or animal is part of more than one food chain. A **food web** shows how one plant or animal is a part of another food chain.

Look at the food chains below. The clover, grasshopper, woodpecker, and owl are part of a food chain. Grasshoppers eat clover. Woodpeckers eat grasshoppers. Owls eat woodpeckers. However, the grasshopper is prey for the woodpecker and for the snake. The grasshopper is part of a second food chain. The second food chain has different plants and animals.

Food Chain 1

clover — grasshopper — woodpecker — owl

Food Chain 2

clover — grasshopper — snake — raccoon

Some animals eat many kinds of plants for energy. Some animals eat many kinds of animals for energy. Some animals fight each other for the same kind of food.

Food Web

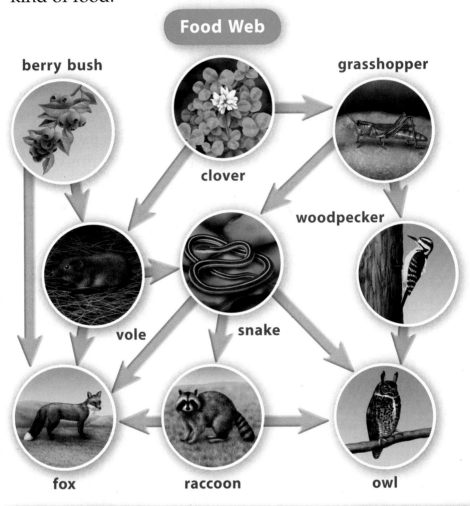

berry bush

clover

grasshopper

vole

snake

woodpecker

fox

raccoon

owl

SEQUENCE

What is the relationship between a predator and its prey?

2

How Is Matter Cycled in an Ecosystem?

Some organisms get energy by eating the remains of dead organisms. These organisms are an important part of an ecosystem.

Scavengers

Predators spend much of their time hunting for prey. However, some animals look for dead animals. These animals are scavengers (SKAV uhn jurs). A **scavenger** is an animal that eats the remains or wastes of other animals.

Scavengers are consumers. They get energy from the food they eat. Scavengers get energy from eating the remains of things that were once alive. Scavengers often eat the remains of prey that was killed by another animal.

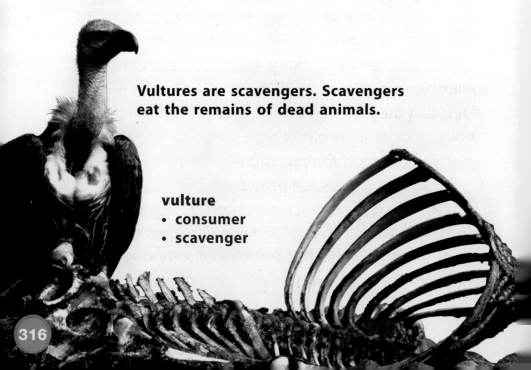

Vultures are scavengers. Scavengers eat the remains of dead animals.

vulture
- consumer
- scavenger

peccary
- consumer
- omnivore
- scavenger

A peccary is an animal that is both an omnivore and scavenger. It eats plants, animals, and the remains of dead animals.

Predators and Scavengers

Predators and scavengers are both carnivores. Predators hunt and kill other animals for food. Scavengers eat what the predators do not eat. For example, a predator such as a wolf kills an animal such as a moose. The wolf does not eat all of the moose. Scavengers eat what is left. Scavengers get energy from food that would otherwise be wasted.

Some scavengers are prey for other animals. When a predator eats a scavenger, energy is passed along in the food chain. This is one reason why scavengers are an important part of a food web. Scavengers are a part of every kind of ecosystem.

Helpful Organisms

Fungi (FUHN jy) and bacteria (bak TIHR ee uh) are organisms. Some kinds of fungi and bacteria can make people sick. However, most fungi and bacteria are helpful.

All organisms die. You know that some dead organisms are eaten by scavengers. But some are not. When some organisms die, their bodies **decay** (dih kay), or break down into simpler parts. Fungi and bacteria are decomposers (dee kuhm POH zurz). A **decomposer** is a living thing that breaks down the remains of dead organisms. All food chains end with decomposers. For example, bacteria and fungi help break down a dead tree. As the tree decays, energy is released into the soil. New living things use this energy to grow.

This dead tree has decomposers, scavengers, producers, herbivores, omnivores, and carnivores living on it.

fungi

beetle

dead tree

ant

salamander

Organisms decay and release energy for new living things to use. This is called recycling (ree SY kuhl ihng). **Recycling** is the process of breaking down things into a different form that can be used again.

Decay happens much faster in places where it is warm and wet. Animals that die in places where it is cold and dry do not decay for a long time.

Decomposers help the environment. They clean up the remains of dead organisms. They recycle valuable energy that other organisms use to grow. Some decomposers are microorganisms. A **microorganism** (my kroh AWR guh nihz uhm) is a tiny living thing that can only be seen with a microscope. Bacteria are one kind of microorganism.

mouse

fern

moss

termites

millipede

soil

Benefits to Plants and Animals

Decomposers are a very important part of ecosystems. They release energy that plants and animals need to stay alive. Decomposers clean up dead organisms. Other living things can live where the dead organisms once were.

Since decomposers are helpful, it is important for decomposers to grow. People can help. They can make the best environment for decomposers. A compost (KAHM pohst) pile is a place set aside for dead organisms to decay.

Compost piles can be made from garbage. Most people throw away food, paper, dead leaves, and grass. These things are good for compost piles.

This compost pile has many dead plants in it.

Many things that people do not want or need are thrown into the garbage. The garbage is taken to landfills. Landfills are large places where garbage is placed. Some things take up a lot of space in a landfill. Many things may not decay very much in a landfill.

Putting dead organisms or things that decay in a compost pile is helpful to the environment. Bacteria and fungi live in great numbers in compost piles. These decomposers help the compost pile decay. Energy is put back into the soil as the compost pile decays. New living things can use the energy to grow.

Food, grass, leaves, and paper can be put in a compost pile. What percent of all the garbage is that?

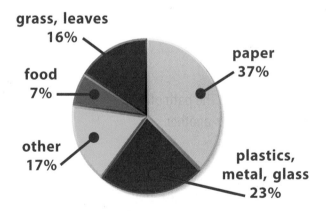

grass, leaves
16%

food
7%

paper
37%

other
17%

plastics,
metal, glass
23%

CAUSE AND EFFECT

What is one way that decomposers are helpful?

Glossary

carnivore (KAHR nuh vawr) An animal that eats only other animals.

decay (dih KAY) To break down into simpler materials.

decomposer (dee kuhm POH zur) An organism that breaks down the remains of dead organisms.

food chain (food chayn) The path of food energy in an ecosystem as one living thing eats another.

food web (food wehb) Two or more food chains that overlap.

Glossary

herbivore (HUR buh vawr) An animal that eats only plants.

microorganism (my kroh AWR guh nihz uhm) A tiny living thing that can only be seen with a microscope.

omnivore (AHM nuh vawr) An animal that eats both plants and animals.

photosynthesis (foh toh SIHN thih sihs) The process plants use to make food.

Glossary

predator (PREHD uh tawr) An animal that hunts other animals for food.

prey (pray) An animal that is hunted for food by a predator.

recycling (ree SY kuhl ihng) The process of breaking down materials into a different form that is used again.

scavenger (SKAV uhn jur) An animal that feeds on the remains of dead animals.

Think About What You Have Read

Vocabulary

1 Which of the following is an animal that eats only other animals?

A) carnivore

B) prey

C) herbivore

D) omnivore

Comprehension

2 Explain how the energy plants make during photosynthesis is passed to predators.

3 What two kinds of organisms get energy from the remains of once-living organisms?

4 Describe the flow of energy in a food web.

Critical Thinking

5 Are human beings herbivores, carnivores, or omnivores? What evidence supports your answer?

Adaptation and Extinction

Contents

How Are Organisms Adapted to Survive?

Plants and animals must adapt to their environment. Adaptations help them get food, hide from predators, and survive.

Plant and Animal Adaptations

Different plants and animals live in different environments. The place where a plant or animal lives is called its **habitat** (HAB ih tat). The habitat of a dolphin is the ocean. The habitat of a cactus is the desert.

Plants and animals have adaptations (ad ap TAY shuhnz). An **adaptation** can be a physical feature or a behavior that helps a plant or animal survive. The webbed feet of a duck are an adaptation that is a physical feature. Hunting at night is an adaptation that is a behavior.

A wood duck's feet are webbed to help it swim.

FOREST
The aye aye sleeps during the day and hunts at night. It has large eyes that help it see at night.

RAINFOREST
Water that stays on leaves can cause disease. Leaves with pointed ends allow water to drip off.

The role a plant or animal plays in its environment is called its **niche** (nihch). A niche includes the kind of food a living thing uses. An opossum's niche includes eating berries at night. Many living things can share a habitat. However, each has its own niche.

young deer

Camouflage

Some animals hide by looking like what is around them. These animals have an adaptation called camouflage (KAM uh flahzh). **Camouflage** is the coloring or marking of an animal that helps it look like what is around them.

Camouflage can help both predators and prey. You know that predators are animals that hunt other animals for food. You know that prey are animals that are hunted.

Look at the young deer's fur. The color and spots help the deer look like its forest habitat. Predators have a hard time seeing it.

An arctic fox is a predator that uses camouflage. Its fur looks like what is around it. Its prey does not see the fox.

arctic fox

Color and Mimicry

Some animals have bright colors. Other animals can see them easily. This adaptation is called warning coloration. The blue poison dart frog stands out. Its bright color warns predators that it is poisonous.

Some animals protect themselves by using mimicry (MIHM ih kree). **Mimicry** is an adaptation where an animal looks like another animal or a plant. Many insects use mimicry. The South American owl butterfly has large spots on its wings. The spots look like the eyes of an owl. These spots scare away birds that might eat the butterfly.

owl

South American owl butterfly

blue poison dart frogs

The kangaroo rat stays in its burrow during the day. This behavior helps it survive the heat of the desert.

Behavior

Behavior can help a predator as it hunts. Wolves and other animals hunt in groups. The group surrounds the prey so it cannot escape.

Behavior also helps prey survive. Rabbits run in a zig-zag pattern. This behavior can help them escape from predators.

Some animals such as bats, frogs, and chipmunks have an adaptation that helps them survive winter. They **hibernate** (HY bur nayt), or go into a deep sleep, during which they use very little energy. This behavior helps the animals get through long, cold winters.

This archer fish can shoot a jet of water. This behavior helps it knock insects into the water where it can eat them.

PROBLEM AND SOLUTION

What are two examples of adaptations that help animals hunt?

What Threatens the Survival of Species?

Plants and animals face a number of threats to their survival.

How Organisms Change Environments

Every living thing causes change in its environment. These changes affect other living things. Some changes are slow to happen. Think of a young tree growing among some flowers. The tree takes many years to grow. As it gets big, the tree will be a home for many living things. However, it will block the sunlight needed by some plants to live.

Other changes happen more quickly. People can change a forest into a city or a river into a lake. To change a river into a lake, people build a dam. The Aswan Dam in Egypt was built to hold back the flood waters of the Nile River.

The Aswan Dam was built in 1970 to control floods.

334

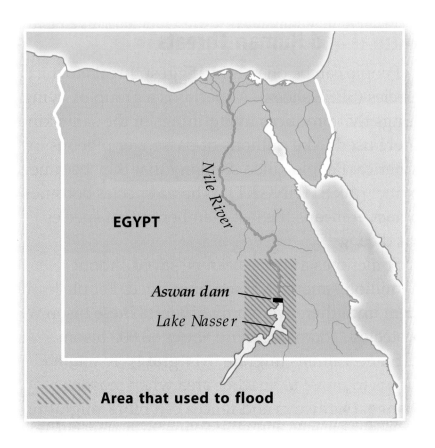

EGYPT

Nile River

Aswan dam

Lake Nasser

Area that used to flood

A change like a dam has good and bad effects. The Aswan Dam has helped people in Egypt. It provides electricity. It has improved travel on the river. It holds back flood waters.

But the dam has done harm, too. Before the dam, flooding left soil rich in nutrients on the river's banks. Now farmers have trouble growing crops without this rich soil. The dam has upset the habitat of many plants and animals. Fish populations in the river are smaller than before.

Some plants and animals can adapt to changes in their habitat. Others cannot. The ones that can adapt have the best chance for survival.

Natural and Human Threats

People can be one of the biggest threats to a species (SPEE sheez). A **species** is a group of living things that produces living things of the same kind. There used to be millions of passenger pigeons in America. People killed so many that they became extinct (ihk STIHNGKT). When a species becomes **extinct**, it means the last member of that species has died.

Sometimes a species can be saved. About 30 million American bison once lived. People hunted them until there were only 750 left. These bison were protected. Today there are about 80,000 bison.

Some animals migrate (MY grayt). To **migrate** means to move to another area when seasons change. Highways and fences can block migrating animals.

CAUSE AND EFFECT

Name one threat to an organism's survival.

American bison

What Do Fossils Tell About the Past?

Scientists study fossils to learn about living things in the past.

Why Scientists Study Fossils

How do scientists know what Earth was like millions of years ago? They study fossils (FAHS uhlz) to get clues. A **fossil** is the preserved remains of an organism that lived long ago. Fossils can include bones, teeth, and shells. A fossil can also be an imprint left in the mud long ago.

Some clues tell scientists how long ago something lived. For example, how deep a fossil is found in a layer of rock is a clue to its age. Other clues tell what an animal ate. For example, fossils of a dinosaur's teeth are clues to what it ate. What kind of food do you think that a dinosaur with sharp teeth ate?

fossil tree fern

This fossil of a fern looks like ferns that live today.

modern fern

Classifying Fossils

A scientist who studies fossils is called a **paleontologist** (pay lee ahn TAHL uh jihst). Part of a paleontologist's job is to classify fossils. This can be difficult because fossils are often only parts of the once living thing.

A paleontologist uses what is known about today's plants and animals to study fossils. Look at the pterosaur (TEHR uh sawr) and bat shown. You can see ways that they are alike. The pterosaur's wings were like a bat's wings. Some of the pterosaur's body was like a bird's. Some of its body was like a reptile's. No sign of feathers has been found on any pterosaur fossils. For this reason, the pterosaur is classified as a flying reptile.

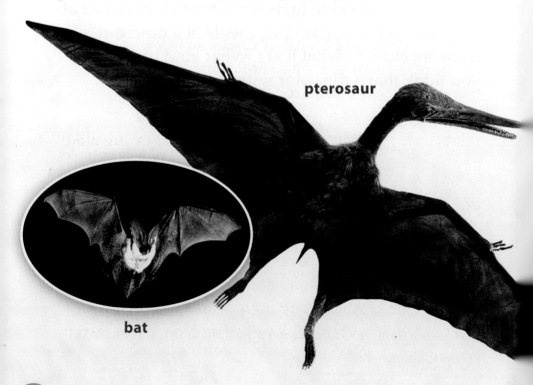

pterosaur

bat

The *Phiomia* was an early
relative of the elephant.

Fossils and the Present

Most species of plants and animals that were
alive millions of years ago are now extinct.
Paleontologists compare fossils of these extinct
species to species alive today. They look for
relationships. They want to know how they are alike
and how they are different.

Today there are only three species of elephant.
However, more than 300 species of elephant have
lived on Earth at some point in time. The *Phiomia*
(fee OH mee uh) was a relative of today's elephant.
It lived about 30 million years ago. It had tusks and
a small trunk. Another relative was the wooly
mammoth. It had huge, long, curved tusks and was
covered with fur.

Dating Fossils

Scientists have made a timeline called the geologic time scale. It shows important events in Earth's history. It gives information about the kinds of organisms that lived at different times. A very simple version of the time scale is shown here.

The time scale is broken into sections called eras (IHR uhz). An **era** is a major section of time. Each era lasted many millions of years.

COMPARE AND CONTRAST

Compare the types of animals that lived in the Cenozoic Era and the Mesozoic Era.

Geologic Time Scale

Many mammals, including people, live during the current era, the Cenozoic Era.

Dinosaurs, including this velociraptor, lived during the Mesozoic Era.

Trilobites lived during the Paleozoic Era.

Cenozoic Era 65 million years ago to present

Mesozoic Era 248–65 million years ago

Paleozoic Era 544–248 million years ago

Glossary

adaptation (ad ap TAY shuhn) A physical feature or a behavior that helps an organism survive in its habitat.

camouflage (KAM uh flazh) The coloring, marking, or other physical appearance of an animal that helps it blend in with its surroundings.

era (IHR uh) A major division of geologic time defined by events that took place during that time.

extinct (ihk STIHNGKT) No longer living. When the last member of a species has died, the species is extinct.

fossil (FAHS uhl) The preserved traces and remains of an organism that lived long ago.

habitat (HAB ih tat) The place where an organism lives.

hibernate (HY bur nayt) To go into a deep sleep during which an animal uses very little energy and usually does not need to eat.

Glossary

migrate (MY grayt) To move to another region when seasons change and food supplies become scarce.

mimicry (MIHM ih kree) An adaptation that allows an animal to protect itself by looking like another kind of animal or like a plant.

niche (nihch) The role a plant or animal plays in its habitat.

paleontologist (pay lee ahn TAHL uh jihst) A scientist who studies fossils.

species (SPEE sheez) A group of organisms that produces organisms of the same kind.

Responding

Think About What You Have Read

Vocabulary

1 Organisms that produce living things of the same kind belong to the same group called a/an

A) species.

B) habitat.

C) environment.

D) ecosystem.

Comprehension

2 Explain why it is important for plants and animals to be adapted to their environment.

3 Why do paleontologists study fossils?

4 Compare camouflage and mimicry. How are they alike? How are they different? Give examples of each.

Critical Thinking

5 How might an ecosystem change if an animal that eats insects becomes extinct?

Index

Credits